The Kennedy Autopsy

Jacob Hornberger

THE FUTURE *of*
FREEDOM FOUNDATION

11350 Random Hills Road
Suite 800
Fairfax, Virginia 22030

ISBN 978-1-890687-236

OL25792943M

Contents

Foreword

By Jacob Hornberger

In 1993, Congress established the Assassination Records Review Board (ARRB), whose mission was to secure the disclosure of long-secret federal documents and records relating to the assassination of President John F. Kennedy. The ARRB was formed in response to the public outcry generated by Oliver Stone's movie *JFK*. The main focus of the outcry was the continued secrecy among federal departments and agencies, particularly the military and the CIA, with respect to the Kennedy assassination.

Douglas P. Horne served as Chief Analyst for Military Records for the ARRB. In 2009, Horne authored one of the finest books ever written on the Kennedy assassination, a five-volume work entitled *Inside the Assassination Records Review Board: The U.S. Government's Final Attempt to Reconcile the Conflicting Medical Evidence in the Assassination of JFK*. Focusing primarily on the U.S. military's autopsy of President Kennedy's body, Horne's book carefully documented how the Kennedy autopsy served to cover up the fact that Kennedy was the victim of a conspiracy, one that consisted of officials within the national-security establishment.

I was so impressed with Horne's book that I wrote a 12-part summary and analysis of it, which was published by The Future of Freedom Foundation, where I serve as president. This book consists of that 12-part article plus two other articles I wrote relating to the JFK autopsy.

Contemporaneously with the release of this book, The Future of Freedom Foundation is also releasing a video lecture by Horne entitled "Altered History: Exposing Deceit and Deception in the JFK Assassination Medical Evidence," which summarizes and updates the findings in Horne's book. I cannot recommend this fascinating video presentation too highly. It is now posted on FFF's website (https://www.fff.org/autopsy-references).

We are also releasing another book, *JFK's War with the National Security Establishment: Why Kennedy Was Assassinated*, which consists of a multipart article by Horne that was published by The Future of Freedom Foundation.

That book explains the motives of the U.S. national-security establishment in removing Kennedy from office.

President Kennedy wrote, "The great enemy of the truth is very often not the lie, deliberate, contrived and dishonest, but the myth, persistent, persuasive and unrealistic."

It would be difficult to find a better description of official conclusions reached about Kennedy's assassination than that.

1

On the afternoon of November 22, 1963, one of the most astonishing events in the history of U.S. law enforcement took place at Parkland Hospital in Dallas. It involved a confrontation between agents of the Secret Service and hospital personnel.

After President John F. Kennedy was declared dead at Parkland Hospital, his body was placed into an expensive bronze, ornate casket that had just been ordered and delivered by O'Neal Funeral Home in Dallas. Agents of the Secret Service immediately took control of the casket and began removing it from the hospital, over the vehement objections of the Dallas County medical examiner, Dr. Earl Rose, who was the hospital's chief of forensic pathology. Rose told the agents that they weren't going anywhere with the casket, at least not until an autopsy had been conducted. Since a murder had just taken place, Texas law required an autopsy to be conducted on the victim's body.

The purpose of an autopsy is to determine how the victim was killed. In the ideal case, it's conducted by a forensics pathologist, one trained in violent deaths. The pathologist carefully examines the shooting victim's body, searches for bullets and removes them, probes bullet holes with rods, has photographs and X-rays taken, and fills out an official autopsy report detailing his findings. In a sense, the victim's body is a crime scene, one that must be carefully preserved, examined, and reported on.

What was the Secret Service's attitude toward Rose? The agents confronting him clearly had one mission — to prevent Texas officials from conducting an autopsy on the president's body and to get it out of Parkland Hospital immediately and delivered to Dallas Love Field, where it would be immediately flown back to Washington, D.C. In his book *Conspiracy of Silence*, Dr. Charles Crenshaw, one of the physicians who had attended to the president's wounds, stated that he had heard the "men in suits" telling hospital pathologists Vernon Stembridge and Sidney Stewart that "they had orders to take the president's body back to Washington, D.C., just as soon as it was ready to be moved, and that there would be no Texas autopsy."

What jurisdiction did the Secret Service have over the president's body? None. At that time, it was not a federal offense to assassinate the president. Thus, when Kennedy was shot and killed, the federal government had no jurisdiction over the matter at all. That, of course, included the Secret Service. Nonetheless, the Secret Service agents at Parkland Hospital made it clear to Parkland Hospital officials that they had absolutely no intention of permitting Texas officials to conduct the autopsy required by law. Brandishing guns, they began screaming and yelling for people to get out of their way. When Rose blocked their way, emphasizing to them that Texas law required the autopsy to be conducted, the agents flew into a fit of loud, angry profanities, exposed their guns, and began forcibly pushing people out of the way as they wheeled the casket out of the hospital.

Here's how Crenshaw described this amazing encounter in his book *Conspiracy of Silence*:

As though on cue, a phalanx of guards poured into Trauma Room 1 just as the coffin was being rolled out. They looked like a swarm of locusts descending upon a cornfield. Without any discussion, they encircled the casket and began escorting the President's body down the hall toward the emergency room exit. A man in a suit, leading the group, holding a submachine gun, left little doubt in my mind who was in charge. That he wasn't smiling best describes the look on his face. Just outside Trauma Room 1, Jacqueline [Kennedy] joined the escort and placed her hand on the coffin as she walked along beside it. I followed directly behind them.

When the entourage had moved into the main hall, Dr. Earl Rose, chief of forensic pathology, confronted the men in suits. Roy Kellerman, the man leading the group, looked sternly at Dr. Rose and announced, "My friend, this is the body of the President of the United States, and we are going to take it back to Washington."

Dr. Rose bristled and replied, "No, that's not the way things are. When there's a homicide, we must have an autopsy."

"He's the President. He's going with us," Kellerman barked, with increased intensity in his voice.

"The body stays," Dr. Rose said with equal poignancy.

Kellerman took an erect stance and brought his firearm into a ready position. The other men in suits followed course by draping their coattails behind the butts of their holstered pistols. How brave of these men, wearing their Brooks Brothers suits with icons of distinction (color-coded

Secret Service buttons) pinned to their lapels, willing to shoot an unarmed doctor to secure a corpse.

"My friend, my name is Roy Kellerman. I am special agent in charge of the White House detail of the Secret Service. We are taking President Kennedy back to the capitol."

"You are not taking the body anywhere. There's a law here. We're going to enforce it."

Admiral George Burkley, White House Medical Officer, said, "Mrs. Kennedy is going to stay exactly where she is until the body is moved. We can't have that ... he's the President of the United States."

"That doesn't matter," Dr. Rose replied rigidly. "You can't lose the chain of evidence."

For the second time that day, there was little doubt in my mind as to the significance of what was happening before me.

"Goddammit, get your ass out of the way before you get hurt." screamed another one of the men in suits. Another snapped, "We're taking the body, now."

Strange, I thought, this President is getting more protection dead than he did when he was alive.

Had Dr. Rose not stepped aside I'm sure that those thugs would have shot him. They would have killed me and anyone else who got in their way. Dr. Kemp Clark wanted to physically detain the coffin, but the men with guns acted like tough guys with specific orders. A period of twenty-seven years has neither erased the fear that I felt nor diminished the impression that that incident made upon me.

They loaded the casket into the hearse, Jacqueline got into the backseat, placed her hand on top of the coffin, and bowed her head. As they drove off, I felt that a thirty-year-old surgeon had seen more than his share for one day.

Imagine that — federal agents threatening to use deadly force on doctors who had just finished trying to save the president's life. That's astonishing. And all to prevent Texas officials from doing their job under Texas law. All to prevent them from conducting an autopsy on the president's body.

Why? Why was the Secret Service so adamant about getting the president's body out of the hospital so quickly and preventing an autopsy from being conducted on it? After all, they could have instead said, "Dr. Rose, we fully understand your position. That is Texas law, and we don't want to interfere with or obstruct Texas law. And we certainly don't want to do anything that will adversely impact a criminal case against whoever committed this dastardly act. We are fully prepared to cooperate with you, wait until you have finished with the autopsy, and then return the body to Washington for the funeral."

Isn't that how we would normally expect law-enforcement officials to conduct themselves?

In any event, the ambulance then took the casket, along with Mrs. Kennedy, from the hospital to Love Field, arriving about ten minutes later at 2:14 p.m.

Surprisingly, President Johnson was still there, despite the fact that he had been taken to Love Field soon after the president had died at 1:00 p.m. After all, don't forget that this was the height of the Cold War. It had been less than a year since the United States had come to the brink of nuclear war with the Soviet Union during the Cuban missile crisis. Wouldn't you think that Johnson would consider that the assassination of President Kennedy might be the first step in a Soviet sneak WMD attack on the United States?

Well, as a matter of fact, Johnson did express such a concern. When Kennedy was declared dead at 1:00 p.m., he asked that the public announcement be delayed until after he had left the hospital and headed to Love Field just in case there was an international conspiracy to attack the United States. He stated to White House press secretary Malcolm Kilduff, "I think I had better get out of here ... before you announce it. We don't know whether this is a worldwide conspiracy, whether they are after me as well as they were after President Kennedy, or whether they are after Speaker McCormack or Senator Hayden. We just don't know." Johnson later wrote, "I asked that the announcement be made after we had left the room ... so that if it were an international conspiracy and they were out to destroy our form of government and the leaders in that government, that [sic] we would minimize the opportunity for doing so."

Apparently, however, Johnson's concern wasn't so pronounced that it caused him to get into the air immediately and return to Washington or go to some secret federal facility for use in emergencies. He was still there at Love Field, more than an hour after leaving Parkland Hospital.

In fact, it gets stranger. As vice president, Johnson had flown in Air Force Two, which was also sitting at Love Field. Immediately after Kennedy was shot, Johnson could have proceeded to Love Field, boarded Air Force Two, and flown off.

He didn't do that. Instead, he waited at the hospital until Kennedy had been officially declared dead. Then, after mentioning the possibility of an international conspiracy, he proceeded to Love Field, where he decided that he should change planes, given that he was now the president and, thus, entitled to use Air Force One. In fact, imagine Mrs. Kennedy's reaction when she later boarded the plane, headed to her bedroom, and found Johnson lying on her bed. Why, Johnson even took the time to ensure that his luggage was transferred from Air Force Two to Air Force One, even though both planes were returning to Washington.

Johnson also took the time to summon a Dallas federal judge to swear him in as president.

All that delay meant that Air Force One was still at Love Field when the ambulance arrived with the casket and Mrs. Kennedy. In fact, it's arguable that the president was actually waiting for the casket, given that the Secret Service agent in charge of Johnson's security had already prepared for the arrival of the casket by removing two rows of seats in the back of the plane.

At 2:47 p.m., one hour and 47 minutes after President Kennedy expired at 1:00 p.m. and Johnson had immediately headed to the airport after expressing concern about the possibility of a foreign attack on the United States, Air Force One, carrying Johnson, Mrs. Kennedy, several other people, and the Dallas casket took off from Love Field and later landed at Andrews Air Force Base.

That connects to the issue of the transportation of Kennedy's body, which I detailed in a November 2010 article entitled, "The Kennedy Casket Conspiracy." That article is included as Appendix A of this book for easy reference. It details the evidence establishing that the president's body was secretly delivered to the Bethesda morgue in a different casket — a cheap gray shipping casket — approximately 1 3/4 hours before the U.S. military's autopsy officially began at 8:15 p.m. "The Kennedy Casket Conspiracy" raises disturbing questions, such as: Who were the officials in dark suits who secretly delivered the president's body in a plain gray shipping casket to the Bethesda morgue? Why was the president's body delivered early to the morgue? What happened to the body between 6:35 p.m. and 8:15 p.m.? Why was it necessary to keep all this secret from the American people (and from Mrs. Kennedy, who, unbeknownst to her, was accompanying an empty casket to the Bethesda morgue)? I invite you also, after reading that, to read "The Shot That Killed Kennedy." This is an article I wrote in August 2011 (included here as appendix B for easy reference), which shows that the hole in the back of Kennedy's head, as observed by the Parkland Hospital doctors immediately after the shooting, was not depicted in the photographs that were taken as part of the U.S. military's autopsy of the president's body.

Did you notice I said, "the U.S. military's autopsy"? That's correct: after preventing the Parkland Hospital personnel from conducting an autopsy of the president's body, an autopsy was actually turned over to the U.S. military to conduct.

Why the military? That's a fascinating question, one that deserves careful examination. After all, what business did the U.S. government itself have in taking control of the autopsy? As I previously noted, the shooting of the president involved no federal crime. Even though it involved the president of the United States, under the law at the time, it was a plain murder case, one governed by the laws of the state of Texas. Yet the federal government simply assumed jurisdiction over the autopsy — and after its agents had threatened to use deadly force to prevent Texas state officials from conducting the autopsy as required by Texas law.

If the federal government was so concerned about an autopsy, why didn't Secret Service agents simply let it be conducted in Texas, as the law required? Why didn't Lyndon Johnson stop the casket from being loaded onto Air Force One and order that it be returned for an official autopsy conducted under state law? Why the urgency of bringing the body back to Washington for an autopsy?

Indeed, why not turn the autopsy over to a medical examiner in Washington or Maryland (where Andrews Air Force Base is located)? After all, the president is a civilian in a country that purports to be run by civilians. Why wasn't the autopsy turned over to a civilian medical examiner rather than to the U.S. military?

Sure, we often hear that the president is the commander-in-chief, but that's misleading. He's first and foremost the president of the United States, and he's not commander-in-chief of the American people. He's commander-in-chief of the U.S. military.

If the president had been a full-time member of the military, or if he had been murdered on a military base, or if he had been killed on the field of battle in the middle of war, then it might have made sense to have the military conduct an autopsy of the body. Instead, his death involved a simple murder case in Texas.

On the flight to Washington, Navy Adm. George Burkley, who had been Kennedy's personal physician, told Mrs. Kennedy that the president's body had to be taken to a hospital to remove any bullets in it and that that should be done in a military hospital for security reasons.

Security reasons? What security? Were they scared that someone might attack the president's body? In that case, why not simply have people guarding it at the hospital during the autopsy? And if an autopsy had to be conducted, why did Secret Service agents prevent an autopsy from being conducted in Dallas? What was so special about the U.S. military that it had to conduct the autopsy?

Burkley gave Mrs. Kennedy two choices for the autopsy — Walter Reed Army Medical Center or the U.S. Naval Medical Center in Bethesda, Maryland. Since her husband had been in the Navy during World War II, she chose Bethesda.

Of course, hardly anyone during that time questioned the fact that the U.S. military was conducting the autopsy. That was a time when there was tremendous deference to authority and unwavering trust in federal officials, especially the military, among the American people. It was before Vietnam, the Gulf of Tonkin, the Pentagon Papers, syphilis experiments, Watergate, and Iran-Contra. Hardly anyone asked, "Why is the military, rather than civilian authorities, conducting the autopsy? Why did they prevent the Dallas officials from conducting the autopsy?" It never occurred to most Americans that their government might be up to no good.

There is no question, however, that military culture played a critically important role in the autopsy of John F. Kennedy's body. Let's examine how.

2

Three of the major things that distinguish military life from civilian life are: deference to authority, obedience to orders, and a penchant for secrecy. All three of those characteristics played an important role in the military autopsy of John F. Kennedy's body.

Throughout their military careers, it is ingrained in soldiers — both enlisted men and officers — to defer to the authority of their superiors and obey their orders. Even when the orders seem to make no sense, soldiers know that their duty is to carry them out anyway, whether they understand their rationale or not.

Consider, for example, John Stringer, an enlisted man who was the official military photographer during the Kennedy autopsy. With the assistance of Floyd A. Riebe, another enlisted man, Stringer's job was to photograph the wounds and any other parts of the body that the pathologists requested.

In November 1966, Stringer was ordered to appear at the National Archives to participate in an inventory of the photographs that had been taken during Kennedy's autopsy. He noticed something odd — the inventory of photographs did not match the photographs that he had taken during the autopsy.

So what did he do? The following is his testimony in a deposition taken before the Assassination Records Review Board (ARRB) in 1996, as recounted in Douglas Horne's book on the Kennedy assassination, *Inside the Assassination Records Review Board* (volume 1, page 206). The questioner is Jeremy Gunn, general counsel for the ARRB:

> **Gunn:** Do you see the phrase, next to the last sentence, of the document — and I'll read it to you: "To my personal knowledge this is the total amount of film exposed on this occasion?" Do you see that?
> **Stringer:** Yes.
> **Gunn:** Is it your understanding that that statement is incorrect?

> **Stringer:** Well, yes. If they say that there were only 16 sheets of film out of [sic] 11, I'd say that's incorrect.
> **Gunn:** When you signed this document, Exhibit 78, were you intending to either agree or disagree with the conclusion reached in the second to last — next to last sentence?
> **Stringer:** I told him that I disagreed with him, but they said, "Sign it."
> **Gunn:** And who is "they." Who said, "Sign it"?
> **Stringer:** Captain Stover.
> **Gunn:** Was Mr. Riebe in the room when you signed this?
> **Stringer:** I don't remember. His signature is on it, so I guess he was there. But I don't remember.

(Capt. John Stover was the commanding officer of the Naval Medical School at Bethesda and was the superior officer of Commander James Humes, one of the three pathologists who conducted the autopsy on the president's body.)

Later in the deposition, Stringer explained that the customary procedure in autopsy photography was to include an identification tag or a ruler in the photograph. Stringer explained that that procedure wasn't being strictly adhered to in the Kennedy autopsy. In his testimony before the ARRB, he explained why he didn't object to this violation of established procedure:

> **Gunn:** Did it really take that much time to put a ruler into a photo?
> **Stringer:** Well, they get it set up and all that. I mean, when they were doing it, they were in a hurry and said, "Let's get it over with."
> **Gunn:** Did you object to that at all?
> **Stringer:** You don't object to things.
> **Gunn:** Some people do.
> **Stringer:** Yeah, they do. But they don't last long.

With those answers, Stringer was emphasizing the deference-to-authority tradition in military culture. Those who make waves — who object to orders — who disclose wrongdoing — who go over people's heads in the chain of command — don't last in the military. Promotions slow up for soldiers who do those sorts of things. Over time, such soldiers are ground out of the system. They're not considered team players. They can't be trusted.

What were the discrepancies between the photographs taken by Stringer and the photographs in the 1966 inventory? There were several. Horne summarizes Stringer's testimony (volume 1, page 182):

> So John T. Stringer, Jr., under oath, told the ARRB that he had taken 5 different photographic views of the body which Jeremy [Gunn] and I knew were not in the official autopsy collection:
> - The full body from above;
> - The interior of the eviscerated chest, up near the neck, after removal of the lungs;
> - The interior of the eviscerated body cavity near the adrenals;
> - The body lying on its stomach; and
> - "Openings" [plural] in the back, while the torso was propped upright as if sitting.

One of the fascinating aspects of the Kennedy autopsy was the high level of secrecy under which it was conducted. In fact, on the morning after the autopsy, the people who had participated in it were ordered to never disclose anything they had witnessed during the autopsy, on pain of military court martial or criminal prosecution. They were also required to sign secrecy oaths in which they swore never to disclose what they had seen.

Stringer described the experience in his ARRB testimony (Horne, volume 1, page 169):

> **Gunn:** Were you ever previously under any kind of order or restraint from being able to talk about the autopsy?
>
> **Stringer:** Yes, I was.
>
> **Gunn:** Can you explain, very briefly, what the nature of the order was or the circumstances that put you under the order?
>
> **Stringer:** Well, I think it was the morning after the autopsy. We were gathered into the commanding officer's office of the Naval Medical School, who through the fear of God and everyone and he had a paper that we all had to sign that we would not talk to anyone about what had happened on that particular night.
>
> **Gunn:** Do you remember the name of the person who gave you the order?
>
> **Stringer:** John Stover.

According to Horne, "It appears that each one of the enlisted men who received one of these letters was warned orally the day after the autopsy, and then was required to sign a written warning, a 'letter of silence,' the following week, formally acknowledging that they had received and understood the order not to talk about the autopsy" (volume 1, pages 169–70).

Some 14 years later, some of those people were still scared to talk, even before the House Select Committee on Assassinations (HSCA), which had reopened the Kennedy assassination, owing to widespread doubts among the American people about the Warren Commission Report. Horne writes (volume 1, page 171),

> Some autopsy witnesses (morgue technicians Paul O'Connor and James Jenkins) were extremely reluctant to talk to them, but ended up doing so in-person; photographer Floyd Riebe and x-ray technician Ed Reed both consented to brief interviews on the phone; while x-ray technician Jerrol Custer demanded the HSCA staff come to see him in person, and then "hung up" on them.

According to Horne, "The military did not give in easily. On November 3, 1977, Deanne C. Siemer of the DOD Office of General Counsel sent a letter to HSCA Chief Counsel Robert Blakey refusing to rescind the order not to talk, since the 'record with respect to the autopsy is complete and has been preserved intact.' After the military realized that Congress, not the military, makes the final decisions in such matters, 'the Surgeon General of the Navy, VADM W.P. Arentzen mailed out letters rescinding the gag order to the last known addresses of the personnel concerned'" (volume 1, page 171). As Horne explains, the impact of the lifting of the military's gag order was enormous (volume 1, page 171):

> Even though the Surgeon General's letter rescinding the order only mentioned freedom to talk to the HSCA, effectively "the lid was off" and "the cat was out of the bag." Once the HSCA published its report and accompanying 12 volumes of evidence in 1979, the public became aware of the names of most of the autopsy witnesses and participants, and when independent researchers began to contact them, most of them then felt free to talk. The HSCA's charter to reinvestigate the assassination "let the genie out of the bottle," and the evidence in the JFK assassination has not been the same since.

Of course, we shouldn't forget that the U.S. military wasn't the only entity that demanded that matters in the Kennedy assassination be kept secret. The Warren Commission ordered that many of its records and much of its evidence be kept secret from the American people for 75 years. The HSCA also had a penchant for secrecy; it ordered many of its records and much of its evidence sealed for 50 years.

In fact, one of the most fascinating things the HSCA ordered to be kept secret for 50 years was the deposition of Robert Knudsen, a civilian who was the official White House photographer for President Kennedy. The deposition, which was taken in 1978, encompasses one of the most mysterious aspects of the Kennedy autopsy. It came to light only because of the 1992 JFK Records Act, which ordered that government records of the Kennedy assassination be disclosed to the public. The law had been enacted after Oliver Stone's movie *JFK* produced a large public outcry over the federal government's continued secrecy in the Kennedy assassination.

By the time the ARRB learned about Knudsen's role in the assassination, he had passed away. However, Knudsen's wife told the ARRB that on the afternoon of the assassination, he received a telephone call — she believed from the Secret Service to go to Andrews Air Force Base to meet the plane from Dallas and accompany the president's body to Bethesda. His wife and kids told the ARRB that "Robert Knudsen had told them he photographed the autopsy of President Kennedy and was the only one to do so" (volume 1, page 249). The ARRB dug up the August 1977 copy of a magazine entitled *Popular Photography*, which contained an interview with Knudsen. The article stated, "When the news of the assassination came from Dallas, Knudsen left the hospital to meet Air Force One at Andrews Field. He was the only photographer to record the autopsy — 'the hardest assignment of my life'" (volume 1, page 250).

Why is that fascinating and mysterious?

As you'll recall, the photographers at the autopsy were John Stringer and Floyd Riebe, not Robert Knudsen. Neither Riebe nor Stringer ever saw Robert Knudsen at the autopsy. Yet Knudsen said that he was the only photographer to record the autopsy.

When Knudsen was deposed by the HSCA, he never mentioned that he had photographed the autopsy, and, equally significant, he was never asked whether he had photographed the autopsy. In fact, as one reads through his testimony, one almost gets the feeling that this was something that he knew should not be discussed and that he would not be asked about.

The deposition focused entirely on his participation in the developing of photographs that had been taken during the autopsy.

So did Knudsen actually take photographs as part of the Kennedy autopsy, or was he lying about it for some unknown reason? Horne thinks that he was telling the truth, which would seem to make sense, given that he had no reason to make up the story and since it would have been easy for U.S. officials to disclose that he — the White House photographer for President Kennedy — was a liar. Horne's theory is that Knudsen took his set of photographs as part of a super-secret, post-autopsy session that Stringer and Riebe were not part of.

Although Knudsen was a civilian, his familiarity with military culture was confirmed in a statement his wife made to the ARRB. According to Horne, she stated that "her husband was a man who did not talk too much, and who very reliably could keep secrets and told me that sometimes people in the military are required to 'take secrets with them to the grave' when ordered to do so by duly constituted authority, regardless of later attempts to get them to talk" (volume 1, page 253).

Knudsen's penchant for keeping secrets was demonstrated during his deposition before the HSCA. HSCA staff member Andy Purdy asked him about photographs that contained probes in Kennedy's body (volume 2, page 266):

> **Purdy:** Where were the entry and exit points?
>
> **Knudsen:** Here again, I have a mental problem here that we were sworn not to disclose this to anybody. Being under oath, I cannot tell you I do not know, because I do know; but, at the same time, I do feel I have been sworn not to disclose this information and I would prefer very much that you get one of the sets of prints and view them. I am not trying to be hard to get along with. I was told not to disclose the area of the body, and I am at a loss right now as to whether — which is right.
>
> **Purdy:** Was it a Naval order that you were operating under that you would not disclose?
>
> **Knudsen:** This was Secret Service. To the best of my knowledge, Dr. Burkley also emphasized that this was not to be disclosed.
>
> (Navy Adm. George Burkley was Kennedy's personal physician).

Knudsen's penchant for secrecy, however, apparently did not extend to his family, at least partially. According to Horne:

> After he was deposed by the HSCA staff in 1978, he told his family (at different times) that 4 or 5 of the pictures he was shown by the HSCA did not represent what he saw or took that night, and that one of the photographs he viewed had been altered. His son Bob said that his father told him that "hair had been drawn in" on one photo to conceal a missing portion of the top-back of President Kennedy's head.... [His wife] further elaborated that the wounds he saw in the photos shown to him in 1988 did not represent what he saw or took.... (Horne, volume 1, page 251).

One of the more interesting aspects of the military autopsy of President Kennedy was the total indifference among personnel at Bethesda to the possibility that there would be a criminal trial of whoever killed Kennedy. The thought of having to testify in a state criminal murder case, in which a prosecutor would be depending on testimony establishing an accurate autopsy, and in which a team of aggressive criminal defense attorneys would be cross-examining everyone involved in the autopsy, just seems never to have entered the minds of the people involved in the autopsy.

Didn't they know that an autopsy is critically important evidence in helping to convict the person who did the shooting? Didn't they know that the prosecutor would be summoning them to testify at trial and depending on the truthfulness and accuracy of their testimony? Wouldn't they want to help the prosecution secure a conviction in the case? Didn't they know that they would be subjected to withering cross-examination by experienced criminal-defense attorneys?

Consider, for example, the problem involving the "chain of custody." In order for the autopsy results to be admitted into evidence at a criminal trial, it would have been necessary to establish a clear "chain of custody" of the body from Dallas to Bethesda to ensure that there were no shenanigans committed on the body with the aim of misleading people as to the cause of death. That's one reason that the medical examiner at Parkland Hospital, Dr. Earl Rose, was so insistent on conducting the autopsy there in Dallas, as the law required. As Rose told Secret Service agent Roy Kellerman and the other Secret Service agents who were attempting to prevent Rose's autopsy, "You can't lose the chain of evidence."

However, "The Kennedy Casket Conspiracy," details that they did lose the chain of evidence by removing the body from the Dallas casket and delivering it early to the Bethesda morgue in a cheap shipping casket. That break in the chain of custody would have undoubtedly prevented the final autopsy report from being admitted into evidence at trial.

None of that seemed to matter to the autopsy personnel that night. One gets the distinct impression that the possibility of a criminal trial in which autopsy participants would have to testify was the last thing on their minds.

After all, when the autopsy was being conducted, Oswald, the accused assassin had already been taken into custody, and he was still alive and in custody on the next day when military officials were ordering autopsy participants to keep their mouths shut forever and requiring them to sign secrecy oaths.

Did the U.S. military honestly think that its secrecy surrounding the autopsy would not be pierced by a team of aggressive criminal-defense lawyers? Did it honestly believe that experienced lawyers would not discover the secret, early delivery of Kennedy's body to the morgue in a cheap shipping casket and the casket shenanigans engaged in after that? Did they honestly believe that an aggressive criminal-defense team would fail to subpoena all the government's records establishing who the "men in suits" were who conducted the early delivery of Kennedy's body in the cheap shipping casket? Or did they simply think that the possibility that the murder case would ever go to trial in the Kennedy assassination was minimal?

Whatever they were thinking, circumstances did turn in their favor when Oswald was murdered, and U.S. officials quickly concluded that he was a lone-nut assassin in a case in which no other suspects would ever be brought to trial. As a result of those factors, U.S. government officials were successful in keeping the circumstances surrounding John F. Kennedy's autopsy shrouded in secrecy for some three decades.

Let's now continue from where I left off in appendix B "The Shot That Killed Kennedy" and examine some more of the unusual occurrences in the autopsy of John F. Kennedy.

3

Once it was determined that the autopsy of John F. Kennedy's body would be conducted at Bethesda Naval Hospital rather than Walter Reed Army Medical Center, Navy Commander James Humes and Navy Commander J. Thornton Boswell were assigned the task of conducting the autopsy. At 8 p.m. that evening, just before the start of the autopsy at 8:15 p.m., Humes telephoned Army Lt. Col. Pierre Finck and requested his assistance with the autopsy. All three of them were trained pathologists but only Finck specialized in forensic pathology, the branch of pathology that focuses on determining the cause of death.

In 1969, New Orleans District Attorney Jim Garrison brought a criminal case against a New Orleans man named Clay Shaw. The state alleged that Kennedy had been killed as part of a regime-change operation on the part of the U.S. military and the CIA, part of whose mission was to remove Kennedy from power and elevate Vice President Lyndon Johnson to the presidency. The state was alleging that Shaw was a CIA operative who had been part of the plot.

At the trial, Finck was called by the defense to testify about the Kennedy autopsy. He testified that Kennedy had been hit by two bullets, one in the head and one through the neck. The headshot is the subject of Appendix B, "The Shot That Killed Kennedy." It deals with the controversy over the U.S. military's official photographs of the back of Kennedy's head, which fail to depict the large hole in the back of his head that physicians at Parkland Hospital observed when they were trying to save the president's life.

The issues involving the neck wound are no less strange, for it is the wound that involves the so-called magic bullet. We'll examine that controversy later, but for now, I'd like to share with you two interesting aspects of Finck's testimony at the Shaw trial in New Orleans.

The first one relates to the points I made in chapter 2. In that chapter, I focused on certain characteristics of military culture: deference to authority, obedience to orders, and a penchant for secrecy. Finck's testimony reflected all three military characteristics.

A standard procedure in autopsy cases is for the pathologist to "dissect" the track of a bullet wound to determine the exact direction that the bullet took and also to help locate the bullet, especially if it came to rest inside the body. Ballistics tests can then be conducted on the bullet to determine whether it was fired from a particular rifle.

That procedure wasn't followed with Kennedy's neck wound, and the prosecutor in the Shaw case, Alvin Oser, wanted to know why it wasn't. The following is from the transcript of Finck's testimony at the Shaw trial. The questioner is Oser:

> **Q:** Did you have an occasion to dissect the track of that particular bullet
>   in the victim as it lay on the autopsy table?
> **A:** I did not dissect the track in the neck.
> **Q:** Why?
> **A:** This leads us into the disclosure of medical records.

Doesn't that seem to be a rather strange answer? Given that Finck's testimony revolved entirely around the autopsy of Kennedy's body, his testimony necessarily involved the disclosure of medical records. Oser refused to let Finck off the hook:

> **Mr. Oser:** Your Honor, I would like an answer from the Colonel, and I
>   would ask the Court to so direct.
> **The Court:** That is correct, you should answer, Doctor.
> **The Witness:** We didn't remove the organs of the neck.

Do you see the problem? Finck still hasn't answered the question. Is he deliberately obfuscating? Or does he honestly think he's answering Oser's question?

> **Q:** Why not, Doctor?
> **A:** For the reason we were told to examine the head wounds and that the —
> **Q:** Are you saying someone told you not to dissect the track?
> **The Court:** Let him finish his answer.
> **The Witness:** I was told that the family wanted an examination of the
>   head, as I recall, the head and chest, but the prosecutors in this
>   autopsy didn't remove the organs of the neck, to my recollection.

Do you see the problem? He's still not answering Oser's question. He's simply repeating that he didn't dissect the organs but he's not answering Oser's question as to *why* he didn't dissect it. If Finck is hoping that Oser will simply give up and move on to another line of questioning, his hope is immediately dashed:

> **Q:** You have said they did not, I want to know why didn't you as an autopsy pathologist attempt to ascertain the track through the body which you had on the autopsy table in trying to ascertain the cause or the causes of death? Why?
> **A:** I had the cause of death.

Do you see that he is still not answering the question?

> **Q:** Why did you not trace the track of the wound?
> **A:** As I recall I didn't remove these organs from the neck.
> **Q:** I didn't hear you.
> **A:** I examined the wounds, but I didn't remove the organs of the neck.

By this time, one has to ask whether Finck is intentionally and deliberately avoiding answering the question.

> **Q:** You said you didn't do this; I am asking you why you didn't do this as a pathologist?
> **A:** From what I recall I looked at the trachea, there was a tracheotomy wound the best I can remember, but I didn't dissect or remove those organs.

But he still hasn't answered Oser's question, has he? So Oser finally turns to the judge for assistance:

> **Mr. Oser:** Your Honor, I would ask Your Honor to direct the witness to answer my question.
> **Q:** I will ask you the question one more time. Why did you not dissect the track of the bullet wound that you have described today, and you saw at the time of the autopsy at the time you examined the body?
> **A:** As I recall I was told not to, but I don't remember by whom.

Finally! There we have it. That's the reason Finck was obfuscating and avoiding answering the question. Army Col. Pierre Finck, the forensic pathologist for John Kennedy's autopsy, was directed not to dissect the track of Kennedy's neck wound to determine the track the bullet had taken, and he obeyed that directive even though it violated standard procedure in autopsy cases:

Q: You were told not to, but you don't remember by whom?
A: Right.
Q: Could it have been one of the Admirals or Generals in the room?
A: I don't recall.

What are the chances that a forensic pathologist, whose responsibility was to dissect Kennedy's neck wound to determine the path of the bullet, is going to forget the identity of the person who has directed him to not do his job in the most important autopsy he'll ever perform in his life, an autopsy of the president of the United States?

I think there's another reason Finck was doing his best to avoid answering Oser's questions and why he very likely committed perjury when he testified that he could not remember the identity of the person who directed him not to dissect the track of the neck wound. My hunch is that Finck had a deep fear of what would happen to him if he revealed the identity of the person who had the power to issue that type of directive during the autopsy, a directive that Finck refused to disobey.

That the three pathologists who conducted Kennedy's autopsy were operating under the authority of a high military official was reinforced by Finck in another part of his testimony during the Shaw trial:

Q: Was Dr. Humes running the show?
A: Well, I heard Dr. Humes stating that — he said, "Who's in charge here?" and I heard an Army General, I don't remember his name, stating, "I am." You must understand that in those circumstances, there were law enforcement officers, military people with various ranks, and you have to co-ordinate the operation according to directions.
Q: But you were one of the three qualified pathologists standing at that autopsy table, were you not, Doctor?
A: Yes, I am.
Q: Was this Army General a qualified pathologist?

A: No.

Q: Was he a doctor?

A: No, not to my knowledge.

Q: Can you give me his name, Colonel?

A: No, I can't. I don't remember.

Elsewhere in his testimony, Finck touched on that part of military culture concerning obedience to orders:

Q: Colonel, did you feel that you had to take orders from this Army General that was there directing the autopsy?

A: No, because there were others, there were Admirals.

Q: There were Admirals?

A: Oh, yes, there were Admirals, and when you are a Lieutenant Colonel in the Army you just follow orders, and at the end of the autopsy we were specifically told — as I recall it, it was by Admiral Kinney, the Surgeon General of the Navy — this is subject to verification — we were specifically told not to discuss the case.

In a memorandum submitted by Finck in 1965 to his commanding officer, Army Brig. Gen. J.M. Blumberg, Finck alluded to another instance of how a superior military official prevented him from doing his job during the autopsy:

I was denied the opportunity to examine the clothing of Kennedy. One officer who outranked me told me that my request was only of academic interest. The same officer did not agree to state in the autopsy report that the autopsy was incomplete, as I had suggested to indicate.

In 1997, the Assassination Records Review Board (ARRB) took the deposition of Navy corpsman Jerrol Custer, who had served as an X-ray technician for the Kennedy autopsy. As I wrote in "The Kennedy Casket Conspiracy," Custer was one of several military personnel who witnessed Kennedy's body secretly being brought into the Bethesda morgue at 6:35 p.m. in a cheap, gray shipping casket rather than the expensive, ornate casket into which the body had been placed in Dallas. ARRB general counsel Jeremy Gunn was the questioner:

Gunn: Was it your impression that Dr. Finck was taking instructions from one or more persons in the gallery, or was he —

Custer: Absolutely.

Gunn: And from whom was he taking instructions?

Custer: From the same two gentlemen that had kept rolling the situation all that night.

Gunn: You've previously referred to that person being a four-star general. Which service was that four-star general with: do you know?

Custer: I'll be honest with you. I can't recollect. All I saw was four big stars. And that was enough.

Gunn: But you're calling him a general. It's, presumably, not an Admiral. I guess that's fair.

Custer: Yes.

Gunn: Presumably, it would be either Army or Air Force?

Custer: Oh, it has to be one of the two. I know an Admiral when I see one. Absolutely. He's got gold halfway up to his elbow.

When Finck was called to testify before the ARRB in 1996, he confirmed that he had received the same type of secrecy order described in Chapter 2. The questioner is Jeremy Gunn, general counsel for the ARRB:

Q: Dr. Finck, did you ever receive any orders or instructions from anyone not to discuss the assassination or autopsy of President Kennedy?

A: At the autopsy, yes.

Q: Can you tell me what the circumstances were around that, who gave you the order for example?

A: As far as I can remember, it was in the autopsy room, and I may have recorded that somewhere, but now the name escapes. I don't remember specifically who told us not to discuss it.

[...]

Q: Would you turn to page 3 of the document that you have in front of you, Exhibit 28. I would like to draw your attention to the paragraph numbered 2 and ask you if that helps to refresh your recollection of any other orders you may have received?

A: Before the Warren Commission, Warren report: "Before the Warren report was published in September '64, I received directives by telephone from the White House through" — something illegible — "through your office."

Q: Your office.

A: "And through the Naval Medical School in Bethesda not to discuss subject autopsy beyond the contents of the Warren report." I don't remember that.

Who was the high military official (or officials) who was directing and controlling the course of the autopsy? To this day, the American people don't know the identity of that person. For almost 50 years, the U.S. military has succeeded in keeping his identity secret. And don't forget, that autopsy room was filled with admirals and generals who were witnessing how the autopsy was being conducted, none of whom has disclosed the identity of that person to the public, confirming that military men do in fact keep secrets very well, especially when they have taken a solemn oath to do so.

At the beginning of this chapter, I said that I wanted to share with you two interesting aspects of Pierre Finck's testimony at the Clay Shaw trial in New Orleans. The first one, just covered, outlines the role that military culture played in the Kennedy autopsy. The second one, which will be detailed in the next chapter, pertains to a portion of Finck's testimony relating to the issues surrounding the multiple deliveries of Kennedy's caskets into the Bethesda morgue prior to the autopsy, as outlined in "The Kennedy Casket Conspiracy." It will be convenient for the reader to read that article in appendix A before my next chapter.

4

In his testimony at the New Orleans trial of Clay Shaw, Lt. Col. Pierre Finck testified as follows:

> When I arrived, X-rays had been taken of [President Kennedy's] head. I had been told so over the phone by Dr. Humes when he called me at home, and I arrived, I would say, a short time after the beginning of the autopsy, I can't give you an exact time, it was approximately 8 o'clock at night.

Do you see the problem? Finck was telephoned by Humes at 8:00 p.m. During that telephone call, Humes advised Finck that X-rays had already been taken of Kennedy's head.

In my article "The Kennedy Casket Conspiracy," I write:

> On December 10, 1963, Lt. Bird filed his official report of the Joint Casket Bearer Team's delivery of the president's casket into the Bethesda morgue on the evening of November 22, 1963. The report stated in part:
>
> > The Joint Casket Team consisted of one officer, one NCO and seven enlisted men (from each branch of the Armed Forces).... They removed the remains as follows: 1. From the ambulance to the morgue (Bethesda) 2000 hours [8:00 p.m.], 22 Nov. 63.
> >
> > (Bracketed material added.)

Do you see the problem?

Consider this timeline:

8:00 p.m. — Official delivery of Kennedy's body in the Dallas casket by the Joint Casket Bearer Team.

8:00 p.m. — Navy pathologist James Humes telephones Army pathologist Colonel Finck to request his assistance with the autopsy and advises him that X-rays of Kennedy's head had already been taken.

Now do you see the problem?

Since the body was officially delivered to the morgue at 8:00 p.m. after it had been transported from Andrews Air Force Base, how is it possible for X-rays of Kennedy's head to have already been taken? As Douglas Horne pointed out in his book *Inside the Assassination Records Review Board*, which is based largely on Kennedy assassination researcher David Lifton's bestselling 1981 book, *Best Evidence*, the only way for X-rays to have been taken prior to 8:00 p.m. was for the body to have been in the morgue prior to the official delivery time of 8:00 p.m.

Thus, in 1969, Lt. Col. Pierre Finck inadvertently corroborated the evidence that would later come out establishing that Kennedy's body had been secretly delivered to the Bethesda morgue at 6:35 p.m. in a plain gray shipping casket, the type used by the U.S. military for transporting bodies during the Vietnam War and wrapped in a black body bag rather than in the white sheets in which it had been wrapped at Parkland hospital.

Consider these excerpts from my article "The Kennedy Casket Conspiracy":

[Navy Chief of the Day Dennis] David added that after his team had delivered the shipping casket into the morgue, he proceeded into the main portion of the hospital, where several minutes later (i.e., at 6:55 p.m.) he saw the motorcade in which Mrs. Kennedy was traveling (and the Dallas casket was being transported) approaching the front of Bethesda Hospital. As he stated to Horne, he knew at that point that President Kennedy's body could not be in the Dallas casket because his team had, just a few minutes earlier, delivered Kennedy's body into the morgue in the shipping casket.

   [...]

In fact, David isn't the only one who saw Mrs. Kennedy's motorcade (which contained the Dallas casket) approaching Bethesda Hospital after the president's body had already been delivered to the morgue at 6:35 p.m. According to Horne, Jerrol Custer told Lifton in 1980 that he had seen Mrs. Kennedy in the main lobby while he was on his way upstairs to process X-rays that had already been taken of the president's body.

                                                   (Horne, volume 4, page 991).

In a 2010 review of volume 4 of Horne's book, David A. Mantik, M.D., Ph.D., a specialist in radiation oncology who has conducted tests on the Kennedy X-rays and determined them to have been altered, provides an excellent synopsis of this portion of Finck's testimony in the context of the casket-delivery controversy set forth by Horne and Lifton:

Finck, as a forensic pathologist, had been asked to assist with the autopsy. As further confirmation for Finck's overall timeline, he arrived (see his Blumberg report) at the morgue at 8:30 p.m. But here is the clincher: during this phone call, Humes told Finck that X-rays had already been taken — and had already been viewed. On the other hand, the official entry time (with the Joint Service Casket Team) was at 8 p.m.! If that indeed was the one and only entry time, how then could X-rays have been taken — let alone developed and viewed (a process of 30 minutes minimum) — even *before* the official entry time? The only possible answer is that the body did not first arrive at 8 p.m.

Furthermore, Custer and Reed, the radiology techs, provide timelines consistent with much earlier X-rays; in particular, they recall seeing Jackie [i.e., Mrs. Kennedy] enter the hospital lobby, well *after* the 6:35 p.m. casket entry — *an entry they had personally witnessed*. In summary, eyewitnesses convincingly support a much earlier timeline than the official entry of 8 p.m. Therefore, multiple casket entries are logically required. And that more relaxed timeline gave H&B [i.e., Humes and Boswell — JGH] time both to perform their illicit surgery and also for skull X-rays to be taken and read, most likely all before 7:30–8:00 p.m.

Thus, as outlined in my article "The Kennedy Casket Conspiracy," we have (1) several Navy enlisted men affirming that Kennedy's body was secretly brought into the morgue in a cheap shipping casket rather than the expensive bronze casket into which the body had been placed in Dallas and in a body bag rather than wrapped in the white sheets from Parkland Hospital; (2) the official written report of Gawler's Funeral Home, which included the notation "Body removed from metal shipping casket at NSNH at Bethesda," and (3) Marine Sgt. Roger Boyajian's official November 26, 1963, security report confirming that the president's casket was carried into the morgue at 6:35 p.m., which was almost one and a half hours earlier than when the body was reintroduced into the morgue at 8:00 p.m. in the Dallas casket. Now we also have an Army colonel who served as one of the three official pathologists for the Kennedy autopsy corroborating that evidence under oath in a criminal proceeding.

Why all of this rigmarole during an official autopsy of the president of the United States? We'll examine that question later, but first let's look at another important aspect of the Kennedy autopsy — the neck wound, the wound that involved the "magic bullet."

5

There is considerable circumstantial evidence indicating that the conclusions reached by the three pathologists in the autopsy of John F. Kennedy were a work in progress, one that was evolving and developing even after the formal autopsy had been concluded and, in fact, even after Kennedy's body had been embalmed and delivered to the White House.

Soon after the assassination, two FBI agents in the D.C. area — Francis X. O'Neill and James W. Sibert — were assigned to meet Air Force One at Andrews Air Force Base, accompany Kennedy's body to the Bethesda morgue, monitor the autopsy, and retrieve any bullet fragments and deliver them to the FBI for ballistics analysis.

O'Neill and Sibert witnessed the autopsy proceedings after they formally began at 8:15 p.m., taking careful notes of what they were seeing and hearing. Four days after the autopsy — November 26, 1963 — they submitted a written report of what they had witnessed, a report that was not included in the Warren Commission Report. In fact, while O'Neill and Sibert were interviewed by Warren Commission staffer Arlen Specter, an interview that left a sour taste in the mouths of both agents, neither of the agents was summoned to testify before the Warren Commission, perhaps owing to what their report contained.

As Douglas Horne documents in detail in *Inside the Assassination Records Review Board*, the O'Neill-Sibert report contained autopsy conclusions that are significantly at variance with what became the final autopsy report. According to the O'Neill-Sibert report, by the end of the autopsy the pathologists had concluded that Kennedy had been hit by two shots, one in the back of the head and one in the back of the right shoulder. In fact, what many people don't realize is that the FBI prepared its own official report on the Kennedy assassination before the Warren Commission submitted its report. The FBI report concluded that two bullets hit Kennedy from behind and one bullet hit Gov. John Connally, who was traveling in the Kennedy limousine (Horne, volume 4, page 1075).

Consider the autopsy "face sheet," which purported to represent the back of Kennedy's body, that J. Thornton Boswell, one of the three official pathologists in the Kennedy autopsy, prepared as part of the official autopsy report. The little black spot near the middle of the back represented Kennedy's back shoulder wound to which O'Neill and Sibert made reference in their report.

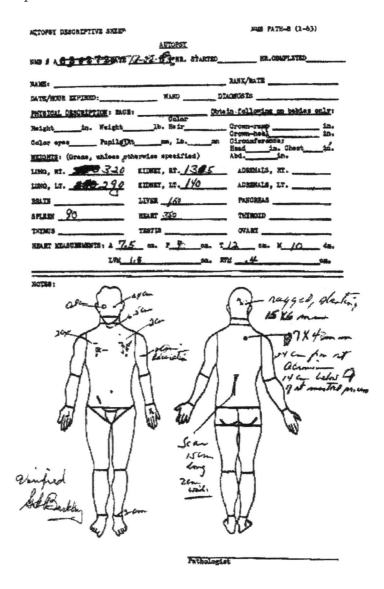

Now consider a photograph of the back of Kennedy's suit, which depicts a hole that seems to line up with the hole depicted in Boswell's autopsy face sheet. (Recall that this was the suit that official autopsy pathologist Col. Pierre Finck was denied access to by an unidentified superior military official during the autopsy, as detailed in Chapter 3).

VIEW OF THE BACK OF PRESIDENT KENNEDY'S
SUIT COAT SHOWING BULLET ENTRANCE HOLE.

EXHIBIT
59

According to Horne, a telex to the FBI from O'Neill and Sibert shortly after they left the Bethesda morgue and their official report dated November 26, 1963, concluded that "the bullet entered the upper back 'just below the shoulders' and 'about two inches to the right of the middle line of the spinal column' and had apparently worked its way out of the president's back at Parkland Hospital while external cardiac massage was being administered during the attempt to save his life."

Secret Service agent Roy Kellerman was in the front passenger seat of the Kennedy limousine in Dallas. In their November 29, 1963, report of their interview with Kellerman, O'Neill and Sibert stated:

Upon turning his head to the left, he [Kellerman] observed President Kennedy with his left hand in back of him appearing to be reaching to a point on his right shoulder.

In volume 4 of his book (page 1039), Horne points to an interview of lab technologist James Jenkins, who participated in the Kennedy autopsy, which was conducted by assassination researcher William Law. Law asked Jenkins whether he recalled the location of the back wound. Jenkins replied:

Probably [reaching around and touching his own back] ... I would say about T-4 [i.e., the level of the fourth thoracic vertebra].

According to Horne (volume 4, page 1039):

Dr. Ebersole confirmed the same estimate of the back wound's location — T-4 — to Dr. David Mantik in a telephone interview before he died. Dr. Burkley identified the location of the entry wound in the back as T-3 in the Navy Death Certificate he filled out and signed. Both of these locations appear to be consistent with the "low" holes in the president's shirt and coat, and with the location of the entry wound made on the body chart by Dr. Boswell at the autopsy.

(Dr. John H. Ebersole, who was present during the autopsy, was assistant chief of radiology at Bethesda Naval Hospital. Dr. Mantik is an assassination researcher. Dr. Burkley, who was present both at Parkland Hospital and during the autopsy at Bethesda, was Kennedy's personal White House physician).

According to Horne, "Autopsy technician Paul O'Connor told interviewer William Law that the back wound was about three inches below the seventh cervical vertebra, and about one or two inches to the right of the spinal column, which appears to be entirely consistent with the vertical placement of this wound given by Burkley and Ebersole."

How deep was the back wound? Not very deep at all, and the evidence indicates that it certainly did not exit the front of Kennedy's body.

When Sibert testified before the Assassination Records Review Board (ARRB) in 1997, he stated (Horne, volume 3, page 699):

But when they raised him up, then they found this back wound. And that's when they started probing with the rubber glove and the finger, and —

also with the chrome probe. And that's just before, of course, I made this call [to the FBI laboratory], because they were at a loss to explain what happened to this bullet. They couldn't find any bullet. And they said, "There's no exit." Finck, in particular, said, "There's no exit." And they said they could feel it with the end of the finger — I mean the depth of this wound....

In 1996, the ARRB interviewed Navy pathologist Frederick Karnei, who was also present at the Kennedy autopsy. According to Horne (volume 3, page 851):

Dr. Karnei said that "about midnight" the prosecutors still had not found a bullet track through the body, nor had they found an exit wound for the entry in the shoulder, and had only a bruise atop the right lung as further evidence of damage.... He said that Humes had concluded that two shots had hit the President from the rear....

In Law's interview, Jenkins confirmed the nontransit nature of the back wound (Horne, volume 4, page 1040):

Humes probed it, to begin with, with his little finger. Humes has big hands. Humes is a big man. And then they used a probe. I could see his finger and I could see the probes behind the pleural area in the back [after the lungs and heart were removed] and it never did break into the pleural cavity. And the wound actually went down and stopped.

Thus, to summarize, by the time FBI agents O'Neill and Sibert left the morgue just before midnight, the official conclusions, according to the O'Neill-Sibert report, seem to have been that Kennedy was shot twice from the back — through the head and in the right shoulder. Although the conclusions didn't address Connally's wounds, the natural inference is that Connally was hit by a third shot.

Soon after the assassination and several hours before the autopsy, law-enforcement personnel found three shell casings on the sixth floor of the Texas School Book Depository, along with the rifle that had supposedly been used in the assassination. Moreover, within an hour and a half of the assassination, law-enforcement personnel had arrested and taken into custody the man suspected of assassinating Kennedy, Lee Harvey Oswald.

Thus, the two wounds described in the O'Neill-Sibert report — two shots into Kennedy, one in the back of the head and one in the back right shoulder that failed to transit through the body — along with a third shot that presumably hit Connally — matched the number of shots supposedly taken by Oswald.

However, sometime after the conclusion of the autopsy and after O'Neill and Sibert had left the morgue, the autopsy pathologists were presented with disquieting information. In a telephone conversation with Parkland Hospital physician Malcolm Perry, who had participated in Kennedy's treatment, Humes learned that there was another wound, a bullet hole through the front of Kennedy's neck. Treating physicians at Parkland Hospital had even announced the existence of the neck wound at a press conference immediately after the president was declared dead. Consider the following portion of that press conference:

Question: Where was the entrance wound?
Perry: There was an entrance wound in the neck. As regards the one on the head, I cannot say.
Question: Which way was the bullet coming on the neck wound? At him?
Perry: It appeared to be coming at him.

Why was that information disquieting? Because a wound in the front of the neck obviously meant a fourth shot — and from the front. Yet Oswald supposedly fired only three shots — and all from the back.

Why hadn't the autopsy pathologists noticed the bullet hole in the front of Kennedy's neck? Because, they said, the wound had been obscured by a tracheotomy that had been performed by the Parkland physicians to help Kennedy breathe. It was only when Perry advised Humes that there was a bullet hole where the tracheotomy was done that the autopsy pathologists realized that they had missed another wound.

The revelation of the neck wound apparently caused considerable consternation in the autopsy room. Recall Finck's testimony at the Shaw trial in New Orleans (as recounted in chapter 3), where Finck testified, with great reluctance, that a high military official, one whose identity he claimed he couldn't remember, instructed him not to dissect the track of the neck wound.

Moreover, in 1977, Boswell made the following cryptic remark to Andrew Purdy, an attorney for the House Select Committee on Assassinations, which had opened an investigation into the Kennedy assassination as a result of widespread public skepticism surrounding the Warren Commission Report: "We got ourselves in dutch with the neck and throat wounds with regard to the Secret Service."

"In dutch" means "in trouble." Why would the pathologists get into trouble with the Secret Service over Kennedy's neck and throat wounds? Indeed, under what authority was the Secret Service even participating in the autopsy, much less apparently chastising the pathologists regarding the bullet wound in the front of Kennedy's neck?

In any event, the pathologists came up with an autopsy report that ended up reflecting a total of three shots, all from behind. We'll examine the fascinating process by which they accomplished that, together with the role that the so-called magic bullet played, in the next chapter.

6

The three military pathologists in the autopsy of John F. Kennedy autopsy, Navy Capt. James Humes, Navy Cmdr. J. Thornton Boswell, and Army Lt. Col. Pierre Finck, were faced with a quandary. After they concluded the autopsy, the number of bullet wounds exceeded the number of shots supposedly taken by the accused assassin, Lee Harvey Oswald.

Initially, the pathologists concluded that Kennedy had suffered two wounds — one to the head and one to the back. Those two wounds, plus Gov. John Connally's wounds, suggested three shots, matching the three shell casings that had been found on the sixth floor of the Texas School Book Depository, from which place Oswald had supposedly taken his shots. (That's assuming, of course, that Connally's multiple wounds were all caused by one shot.)

But after the autopsy was concluded (and after FBI agents Frank O'Neill and Jim Sibert had left the morgue), Humes learned from Parkland Hospital physician Dr. Malcom Perry, who had helped try to save the president's life in Dallas, that there was another bullet wound, this one in the front of the neck. That made a total of four shots to be accounted for and, even worse, the neck wound implied that someone had shot the president from the front.

Humes came up with a way to resolve the problem, although his hypothesis did not make it into the final autopsy report. He posited that Kennedy's wound in the front of his neck had been caused by a bullet fragment from the bullet that was thought to have hit him in the head.

There is a reference to Humes's hypothesis in a transcript of an executive session of the Warren Commission that was held on January 27, 1964, a transcript that the commission classified as "top secret." In *Inside the Assassination Records Review Board* [AARB], Douglas Horne quotes the following excerpt from that top-secret document (Horne, volume 3, page 865; J. Lee Rankin was staff director of the Warren Commission and Rep. Hale Boggs was a member of the Warren Commission):

Mr. Rankin: Then there is a great range of material in regard to the
wounds, and the autopsy and this point of exit or entrance of the
bullet in the front of the neck, and that all has to be developed much
more than we have at the present time. *We have an explanation there
in the autopsy that probably a fragment came out the front of the neck ...*
and the bullet, according to the autopsy didn't strike any bone at all,
that particular bullet, and go through.... [Horne's emphasis.]

Rep. Boggs: I thought I read that bullet just went in a finger's length.

Mr. Rankin: That is what they first said....

A partial transcript of this top-secret Warren Commission executive
session is available on the website of the Mary Ferrell Foundation (for links
to sources, see https://fff.org/autopsy-references).

So under this scenario, the three military pathologists again thought
the wounds accounted for the three shots supposedly fired by Oswald — one
to Kennedy's back and one to his head (which exploded a fragment through
the front of his neck, i.e., his throat) — and then the one that hit Connally,
for a total of three.

The theory that a bullet fragment had exited the neck, however, never
made it into the final autopsy report, for two possible reasons:

One, the Dallas doctors had unequivocally stated that the wound in
the front of Kennedy's neck reflected an entry of a bullet, not the exit
of a bullet fragment. That is, the wound was a small round hole, which
indicated that a bullet had entered from the front. In a press conference
on the afternoon of the assassination, Parkland physician Perry was
unequivocal:

Question: Where was the entrance wound?

Perry: There was an entrance wound in the neck. As regards the one on
the head, I cannot say.

Question: Which way was the bullet coming on the neck wound? At him?

Perry: It appeared to be coming at him.

Perhaps more important, however, was the film of the assassination that
Dallas businessman Abraham Zapruder had taken with his home movie
camera. Zapruder's film established that the president raised his arms in
response to the neck wound before he was hit by the fatal headshot. Thus,
since the neck wound came first and the headshot second, there was no

possibility that the bullet that hit Kennedy in the head exploded a fragment that exited through the front of his neck.

Although the Bethesda pathologists had not seen the Zapruder film, the FBI, the Secret Service, and the CIA all had copies of it during the weekend of the assassination. The FBI had acquired it from Zapruder on the day of the assassination. According to Horne, ARRB investigations in 1997 established that the Secret Service delivered a copy of the Zapruder film to the CIA's top-secret photographic processing center at a Kodak plant in Rochester, New York, during the weekend of the assassination (Horne, volume 4, pp. 1221–43).

While there is no direct evidence that the Secret Service advised the Bethesda pathologists that their theory that a bullet fragment had exited Kennedy's neck would not work, the possibility certainly exists, given that the Secret Service was playing a major role in the autopsy. As I indicated in Chapter 5, Boswell stated that the three pathologists had gotten "in dutch" (i.e., into trouble) with the Secret Service over their handling of the neck wound. Moreover, don't forget that Secret Service agents Roy Kellerman and William Greer had handled the second of the three Kennedy casket deliveries into the Bethesda morgue, as detailed in my article "The Kennedy Casket Conspiracy." In any event, the theory that a bullet fragment from the head exited the front of Kennedy's neck was obviously abandoned, because it never made it into the final autopsy report.

So the pathologists were back to square one: four bullets — one in Kennedy's back, one through his head, one in the front of his neck, and one in Connally — while only three shots were thought to have been taken by Oswald.

Humes resolved the matter by discovering a new wound after the departure of FBI agents O'Neill and Sibert. The newly discovered wound was in the back of Kennedy's neck, which seems to have transited through the neck, exiting from the front. That conclusion was expressed in an interview conducted in 1978 by the House Select Committee on Assassinations of Army 2nd Lt. Richard Lipsey, who served as military aid to the commanding general of the Military District of Washington, Gen. Philip C. Wehle. According to Horne (volume 3, page 857):

> The autopsy conclusions Lipsey was privy to can be summarized as follows: President Kennedy was shot three times from behind (not twice, as Dr. Humes was quoted as concluding prior to midnight by the FBI in its

reports).... The head shot entered the back of the head.... A second bullet entered very high up on the back of the neck and exited from the throat.... A third bullet entered at the bottom of the neck, or high in the back, and did not exit.

So the numbers now matched up — well, except for Connally's wounds. There was Kennedy's head wound, his neck wound caused by a bullet that was supposed to have entered from the back of his neck and exited through his throat, and the back wound. But Connally's wounds obviously still meant a fourth shot.

A solution was ultimately offered by Warren Commission attorney Arlen Spector, who came up with the theory that became famous as the "magic bullet" theory. According to the magic-bullet theory, Oswald fired his gun in a right-to-left trajectory, and the bullet went through the back of Kennedy's neck, exited the front of his neck, turned right to enter Connally's back, crushed a rib, exited the front of Connally's chest, went through his wrist, and lodged in his thigh, after which it plopped out of his leg and deposited itself on Connally's gurney, where it was later found by a hospital employee.

What was magical about the bullet was not simply its trajectory but also the fact that after doing so much damage to Kennedy and Connally, it ended up in virtually pristine shape. In fact, the bullet was only slightly damaged at the base of the bullet. Here's a picture of what has also become known as the "pristine bullet":

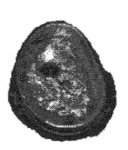

Perhaps most magical of all, however, was the fact that not one trace of flesh or blood was found on the bullet.

Needless to say, it would be difficult to find a more magical bullet than that. It comes as no surprise that experimental tests conducted with similar bullets under similar circumstances have never been able to reproduce the pristine quality of the magic bullet. Such tests have always ended up with mangled bullet fragments, which is what we should expect, given the hardness of people's ribs and wrist bones. As Horne points out, however, bullets fired into water have produced bullets similar in condition to the magic bullet, including the absence of blood or flesh on the bullet.

Unfortunately for the Bethesda military pathologists, however, their problems over the number of wounds in Kennedy's body weren't over. On the day after the assassination — and after the body had already been embalmed and delivered to the White House — the news media were reporting that a bystander during the assassination — James Tague — had been hit in the face by another bullet that had ricocheted off a street curb. Even worse, photographs were being published showing Tague's bleeding face.

Do you see the problem?

That meant, once again, that there were four shots to account for — one to Kennedy's head, one to his back, one through his neck (that was postulated to have hit Connally), and now, the one that hit Tague.

But Oswald was said to have fired only three shots.

How did the military pathologists resolve this new problem? We'll examine that in the next chapter.

7

In chapters 5 and 6 of this book, I described how the autopsy findings with respect to the number and types of wounds on President Kennedy's body were evolving, even after the formal autopsy had been concluded and even after President Kennedy's body had been embalmed and sent to the White House.

I wish to clarify an important point, however. In those two chapters, I stated that these evolving autopsy findings were the result of the three military pathologists' attempting to match the number of wounds with the three bullets that had allegedly been fired by Oswald.

Actually, however, I should have clarified that that's what *appeared* to be happening. There is certainly no direct evidence, as far as I know, of the pathologists overtly saying, "We need to get down to three shots because that's how many shots were allegedly fired in Dallas." Instead, I should have made it clear that that is what it appears they were doing.

This is something I'll return to in a later chapter in this book, but it obviously is an important point that needed to be clarified now.

Let's now return to the evolution of the autopsy findings with respect to Kennedy's back and neck wounds.

Upon discovering that bystander James Tague had been wounded by a separate bullet, the Bethesda military pathologists, James Humes, J. Thornton Boswell, and Pierre Finck, were now confronted with four bullet wounds — one in Kennedy's head, one in the back of Kennedy's neck (which supposedly transited through the front of Kennedy's neck and hit Gov. John Connally as well), the one in Kennedy's back near the right shoulder, and the Tague wound.

That's four shots. So, what did the pathologists do? They simply caused the back wound to disappear, the one that had not transited through the body. Or, to put it another way, they simply merged the back wound and the neck wound into a single wound, one that purportedly hit Kennedy in the back of the neck and exited the front (and then allegedly hit Connally).

That meant three wounds — the head wound, the neck wound (which supposedly hit Connally too), and Tague's wound. (This now matched the number of shots purportedly made by Oswald.)

Humes later testified that he burned copies of his autopsy notes and the initial draft of his autopsy report because, he said, they contained bloodstains on them. But he was unable to explain why he didn't, at the same time, burn Boswell's notes, which also contained bloodstains.

The obvious question arises: Is the more likely reason Humes destroyed such important documents that they reflected the struggles and ordeals the pathologists were undergoing to match the number of wounds with the number of shots purportedly made by Oswald (the subject that we'll be returning to in a later chapter of this book)?

Interestingly, the matter of the disappearing back wound came back into the mainstream news as a result of long-suppressed documents that were liberated by the Assassination Records Review Board, the board that had been established in the wake of the controversy raised by Oliver Stone's movie *JFK*. According to a 1997 Associated Press article on the controversy, the documents revealed that "thirty-three years ago, [Warren Commission member] Gerald R. Ford took pen in hand and changed — ever so slightly — the Warren Commission's key sentence on the place where a bullet entered John F. Kennedy's body when he was killed in Dallas." (Brackets added.) The article states:

> The staff of the commission had written: "A bullet had entered his back at a point slightly above the shoulder and to the right of the spine."
>
> Ford suggested changing that to read: "A bullet had entered the back of his neck at a point slightly to the right of the spine."
>
> The final report said: "A bullet had entered the base of the back of his neck slightly to the right of the spine."

It was not the only time that Ford behaved unusually as a member of the Warren Commission. As the *Washington Post* reported in 2008, a confidential FBI file released that year revealed the extent to which Ford had been acting as a secret liaison to the FBI during his tenure on the Warren Commission, secretly divulging communications within the Commission to the FBI — communications that were being kept secret from the American people. The *Post* article pointed out:

December 1963 memo recounts that Ford, then a Republican congressman from Michigan, told FBI Assistant Director Cartha D. "Deke" DeLoach that two members of the seven-person commission remained unconvinced that Kennedy had been shot from the sixth-floor window of the Texas Book Depository. In addition, three commission members "failed to understand" the trajectory of the slugs, Ford said. Ford told DeLoach that commission discussions would continue and reassured him that those minority points of view on the commission "of course would represent no problem," one internal FBI memo shows.

An obvious question arises with respect to the neck wound.

On the surface of things, the failure of the military pathologists to discover the wound in the front of Kennedy's neck during the autopsy seems plausible. Since the wound was obscured by the tracheotomy that the Dallas surgeons had performed on top of the bullet hole in the front of the neck, one can understand why the military pathologists might have missed the bullet hole.

However, how is it possible for them to have missed the purported wound on the back of the neck — the supposed neck wound that ended up serving as the entry point for the bullet that supposedly exited through the front of the neck? The three military pathologists obviously inspected the back of Kennedy's body. Thus, if an entry wound were there on the back of the neck, it would seem that they would have seen it and stuck a probe all the way through to the front of the neck. Instead, throughout the autopsy, all they supposedly found was the back shoulder wound, a wound that did not transit through the body.

In 1997, the ARRB conducted an interview with Audrey Bell, who was one of the Parkland Hospital nurses. According to Douglas Horne:

> She told us that when she saw Dr. Perry Saturday morning, November 23, 1963 at Parkland Hospital, she told him that he "looked like hell," or words to that effect. She said he told her that he had not gotten much sleep because people from Bethesda Naval Hospital had been harassing him all night on the telephone, trying to get him to change his mind about the opinion he had expressed at the Parkland Hospital press conference the day before, namely that President Kennedy had an entry wound in the front of his neck (Horne, volume 2, page 645).

Moreover, take a look at the following [Warning: grisly photograph] autopsy photograph of the front neck wound. Do you see why the pathologists might have failed to see a bullet hole there?

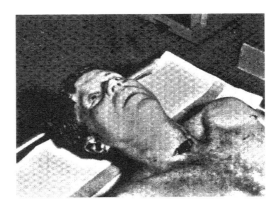

The problem, however, is that, as with Kennedy's head wound, (see my article "The Shot That Killed Kennedy"), the evidence indicates that the appearance of the tracheotomy wound in that photograph was dramatically different at Parkland Hospital in Dallas. According to Horne,

> The article written by Dr. Charles Crenshaw for the anthology Assassination Science (1998) states on page 54, "The wound which I saw after Dr. Perry concluded his work looked nothing like what I saw [referring to the bootleg autopsy photos] in the photographs taken at Bethesda. Dr. Perry had made a very small and neat transverse incision. I took it to be about one to one-and one-half inches on length. It was certainly not of the length I saw in the autopsy photos. The gaping nature of the wound was also inconsistent with what I saw. When the body left Parkland, there was no gaping, bloody defect in the front of the throat, just the small bullet hole and the thin line of Perry's incision...." On page 57, he summarized, "Photographs of President Kennedy's throat show a defect more than twice as long as the tracheostomy incision I remember and more than twice the length these doctors [my colleagues in trauma room one] had earlier estimated [in interviews with author David Lifton] (Horne, volume 3, page 671; brackets in Horne).

Why would someone have tampered with the neck wound? Why would someone have made the tracheotomy gash much larger than it was in Dallas?

Indeed, why wouldn't Navy Admiral George Burkley, Kennedy's personal White House physician, who was present at the autopsy, have advised the Bethesda pathologists of the bullet wound in the front of Kennedy's neck, given that Burkley was present in the emergency room when the Parkland hospital physicians performed the tracheotomy? Don't forget — Burkley was the one who signed the death certificate in Dallas, which stated that Kennedy "was struck in the head by an assassin's bullet and a second wound occurred in the posterior back at about the level of the third thoracic vertebra."

Horne points out that in a 1988 documentary about the Kennedy assassination, *The Men Who Killed Kennedy*, autopsy technician Paul O'Connor, who participated in the autopsy, stated:

> I remember that Dr. Humes was just about ready to pull his hair out, because he was a very meticulous person, and he'd start to do something, and Admiral Burkley would say, "Don't do that!" — and he'd just tense all up and we'd have to go to some other procedure. And I thought to myself, "This is a very strange night." I thought I was in some kind of horror story that was real. But what really scared me was about several days later, after the autopsy, we were ordered into the Commanding Officer's office — all of us that had anything to do with the autopsy, where we signed orders that stated "under penalty of general court martial, you will not divulge any information, or talk to anybody" — that's what scared me. There were kind of mysterious civilian people in civilian clothes [that] were there — it seemed like they commanded lots of respect and attention — sinister looking people. They would come up and look over my shoulder or look over Dr. Boswell's shoulder, and run back and they'd have a little conference in the corner, and then all at once, there's word [that would] come down and says: "stop what you're doing and go to the other procedure" (Horne, volume 4, page 1017).

If all this seems somewhat strange to you, welcome to the club. But you haven't seen anything yet. Wait until you read the next chapter when we return to Kennedy's head wound.

8

One of the most fascinating aspects of the U.S. military's autopsy of President John F. Kennedy's body concerns the examination of Kennedy's brain. The overwhelming weight of the circumstantial evidence establishes that (1) there were two separate brain examinations and (2) the brain that was examined the second time was not that of John F. Kennedy.

A detailed account of this evidence is found on pages 35–47 of volume 1 (JFK's Post-Autopsy Brain Exam: A Major Deception) and in chapter 10 (Two Brain Examinations Coverup Confirmed) of volume 3 of Douglas Horne's book *Inside the Assassination Records Review Board*.

It was Horne and ARRB general counsel Jeremy Gunn who made the discovery of the two separate brain examinations. Horne explains the significance of the discovery:

> This discovery is the single most significant smoking gun indicating a government coverup with the medical evidence surrounding President Kennedy's assassination, and is a direct result of the JFK Records Act, which in turn was fathered by the film, *JFK*. Without Oliver Stone's movie, and the legislation generated as a response to the controversy engendered by the film, this discovery would not have been possible. The JFK Act forced the release, in August 1993, of the HSCA [House Select Committee on Assassinations] staff's previously withheld medical witness interviews; when these previously suppressed interviews were liberated, and married with Hume's Warren Commission testimony and Dr. Finck's summary reports to General Blumberg, the timeline indicating that two separate brain examinations took place became blatantly obvious to me. Without the HSCA interview reports, my hypothesis would never have been formulated. Furthermore, the JFK Records Act created the ARRB, and it was our depositions of Drs. Humes, Boswell, and Finck; photographer John Stringer; and former FBI agent Francis O'Neill as well as our unsworn interview of mortician Tom Robinson that confirmed my suspicions, and

transformed a hypothesis into incontrovertible fact (Horne, volume 3, page 778; information in brackets added).

Keep in mind that the HSCA had ordered that much of its records be kept sealed from the American people for 50 years and that prior to that the Warren Commission had ordered much of its records be kept sealed from the American people for 75 years. The JFK Records Act, which was enacted in the wake of Oliver Stone's movie, brought an end to those orders of secrecy.

Moreover, as I pointed out in chapter 2 of this book, Horne points out that even after the HSCA officially released military personnel who had participated in the autopsy from the oaths of secrecy that the U.S. military had required them to sign immediately after the autopsy:

> The military did not give in easily. On November 3, 1977, Deanne C. Siemer of the DOD Office of General Counsel sent a letter to HSCA Chief Counsel Robert Blakey refusing to rescind the order not to talk, since the record with respect to the autopsy is complete and has been preserved intact.

After the military came to the realization, however, that Congress, not the military, makes the final decisions in such matters, the Surgeon General of the Navy, VADM W.P. Arentzen mailed out letters rescinding the gag order to the last known addresses of the personnel concerned (Horne, volume 1, page 171).

The ARRB's discovery of the two separate brain examinations in the Kennedy autopsy was reported in the following two articles published in 1998 in the *Washington Post*:

"Newly Released JFK Documents Raise Questions About Medical Evidence" by Deb Riechmann (Associated Press, November 9, 1998).

"Archive Photos Not of JFK's Brain, Concludes Aide to Review Board" by George Lardner Jr. (*Washington Post*, November 10, 1998).

The evidence indicates that the first brain examination took place within a few days of Kennedy's assassination, most likely on the morning of Monday, November 25, the day of Kennedy's funeral, and that the second brain examination took place a week or more after the assassination.

What led Horne and Gunn to conclude that there had actually been two brain examinations rather than only one, as reflected in the official autopsy record?

Among the several factors leading to the discovery, as detailed in the section of Horne's book referenced above, were the following five:

First, testimony by the attendees at the brain examinations indicated that there were two separate examinations.

Navy photographer John Stringer (who had been the official photographer for Kennedy's November 22 autopsy) confirmed that he was present at the brain examination but denied that Army pathologist Pierre Finck was there. Finck, on the other hand, confirmed that he too was present at the brain examination but denied that Stringer was there.

That caused Horne and Gunn to suspect that there were actually two separate brain examinations, one that included Stringer and a later one that included Finck. Both examinations involved Navy pathologists James Humes and J. Thornton Boswell (who, along with Finck, had been the official pathologists for Kennedy's November 22 autopsy).

Second, the timeline of the brain examinations indicated that there were two separate examinations.

In an interview conducted by the HSCA in 1977, Boswell stated that the brain examination took place two or three days after the November 22 autopsy. When the HSCA interviewed Stringer, he too stated that the brain had been examined two or three days after the autopsy. In his testimony before the ARRB, Humes stated that the brain examination had occurred one or two days after the autopsy.

However, in a 1965 report to U.S. Army Brigadier General Joseph Blumberg, Finck wrote, CDR Humes called me on 29 Nov 63 that the three prosecutors would examine the brain at the Naval Hospital.

When the ARRB deposed Finck, he testified as follows:

> **Gunn:** Again, I am not asking you to tell me exactly, but I'm just asking whether you remember whether it was within a day or two or whether it was within a week or two?
>
> **Finck:** Oh, it was not a day or two. That's too short.
>
> [...]
>
> **Gunn:** Drs. Humes and Boswell, when they testified to the Review Board, had an initial recollection that they had done a supplementary examination within two or three days after the autopsy. There is no evidence that you were present as far as I am aware in a supplementary examination within two or three days after the autopsy. Do you have

any knowledge whether there was more than one supplementary
examination of the brain?

Finck: [frowning, looking deeply troubled] No. (Horne, volume 3, page
795; brackets in original).

Third, testimony regarding the sectioning of the brain was different.

Stringer testified that at the brain examination he attended, the brain
had been cut into sections to determine the track of the bullet, which is
the standard operating procedure for autopsies. Finck, on the other hand,
stated that there was no sectioning of the brain at the brain examination
that he attended.

Consider the following testimony by Stringer before the ARRB:

Gunn: What happened during the supplementary exam, if you could
describe the process?

Stringer: They took it out, and put it on the table, and describe it [sic] as
to the condition, too some sections of it. We took some pictures of it.
I had a copy board there with the light coming down from the well,
from underneath and with the lights down on it, and shot pictures of
the brain.

Gunn: As it was being sectioned?

Stringer: Yes.

Gunn: Were the sections small pieces, or cross sections of the brain?

Stringer: If I remember, it was cross sections.

Gunn: And what was the purpose of doing the cross section of the brain?

Stringer: To show the damage (Horne, volume 3, page 785).

As Horne points out, Finck, on the other hand, wrote in the Blumberg
Report that the brain he examined was not serially sectioned.

Fourth, the photographs of the brain in the official autopsy records were
not the photographs taken by Stringer during the brain examination that
he photographed.

Consider this testimony by Stringer before the ARRB:

Gunn: Based upon these being basilar views of a brain and based upon
there being no identification cards, are you able to identify with
certainty whether these photographs before you are photographs of
the brain of President Kennedy?

Stringer: No, I couldn't say that they were President Kennedy's. I mean, there's no identification. All I know is, I gave everything to Jim Humes, and he gave them to Admiral Burkley.

[...]

Gunn: Okay. When you took the black and white photographs of the brain of President Kennedy, did you use a press pack?

Stringer: No.

Gunn: Can you identify from the negatives in front of you whether those photographs are from a press pack? And I'm referring to numbers 9, 21, and 22.

Stringer: I think they are. Yes.

Gunn: Would it be fair to say, then, that by your recollection, that the black and white negatives in front of you now were not taken by you during the supplementary autopsy of President Kennedy?

Stringer: Correct. This is Ansco.

Gunn: When you say, This is Ansco, what do you mean?

Stringer: This is Ansco film.

Gunn: What is Ansco film?

Stringer: Well, it's a super high pan. And I think it's from a film pack.

[...]

Gunn: Did you ever use Ansco film yourself in conducting medical photography?

Stringer: Not very often.

Gunn: Did you use Ansco film in the taking the autopsy

Stringer: Not as far as I know.

Gunn: — photographs of President Kennedy?

Gunn: Not as far as I know (Horne, volume 3, pages 806–809).

Horne summarizes the significance of Stringer's testimony regarding the photographs of the brain:

Summarizing, John Stringer testified that the brain photographs in the Archives could *not* be the ones he took because (1) the black and white negatives placed before him at the deposition were numbered proving that there were from a film pack instead of unnumbered, as were all of the portrait pan duplex films he remembered using; (2) the black and white negatives shown to him had no identifying notches in the corner of each negative, as all portrait pan negatives should have had; (3) the color positive transparency images of a brain in the Archives did not have the same identifying notches in the corner of each slide that the Ektachrome E3 slides did; (4) the official collection of brain photographs contained basilar, or inferior views of the intact brain, whereas he did not shoot any basilar views of President Kennedy's brain; and (5) the deed-of-gift brain photographs did not contain any images of serial sections, which in 1996 he vividly remembered seeing dissected, and which he remembered photographing himself at the brain examination, using a light box.

(Horne, volume 3, page 810).

Fifth, the condition of the brain, as depicted in the official photographs, is inconsistent with the actual damage to the brain caused by the headshot.

As Horne points out, the average weight of a normal male brain is about 1350 grams (Horne, volume 3, page 833). But the Supplementary Autopsy Report, as well as Finck's official report to General Blumberg, reported the weight of Kennedy's brain to be 1500 grams.

Why is that a problem?

Because most everyone concedes that a large portion of Kennedy's brain was blown out by the headshot that ended his life. Thus, even with the increase in weight from the solution in which the brain was stored, it's not enough to make up for the large amount of brain mass lost as a result of the bullet that blasted through Kennedy's head.

Horne points out that one of the physicians who treated Kennedy at Parkland Hospital, Dr. Robert McClelland, estimated under oath, in 1964, that at least one-third of the brain was missing when President Kennedy was treated at Parkland Hospital.

When former FBI agent Francis X. O'Neill, who was present during the autopsy, saw the brain outside the cranium, he estimated the percentage of missing brain to be much higher, as reflected in the following testimony he gave before the ARRB:

Gunn: Do you have any sense of what percentage of the brain was missing at the time it was removed from the cranium?

O'Neill: I'm saying this now, 38 years afterwards or something like that 33 years afterwards, 34 years afterwards. It was Oh, well more than half of the brain was missing.

[...]

Gunn: Okay. Could we now see the eighth view, what has been described as the basilar view of the brain, color photograph no.46. And let me say, in the way of preface, these photographs have been identified as having been taken of President Kennedy's brain at some time after the autopsy after they had been set in formalin. Can you identify that in any reasonable way as appearing to be the what the brain looked like of President Kennedy?

O'Neill: No.

Gunn: In what regards does it appear to be different?

O'Neill: It appears to be too much.

Gunn: Could we now look — Let me ask a question. If you could elaborate a little bit on what you mean by it appears to be too much?

O'Neill: ... This looks almost like a complete brain. Or am I wrong on that? I don't know.... In all honesty, I cannot say it looks like the brain I saw, quite frankly I — As I described before, I did not recall it being that large. If other people say that this is what happened, so be it. To me, I don't recall it being that large (Horne, volume 3, pages 815–817).

Why was the brain examination so important in the Kennedy autopsy? Because by tracking the damage done by the bullet, the brain examination could detect whether the bullet entered from the front or from the back of Kennedy's head. The official autopsy photographs of what purports to be Kennedy's brain, the photographs that Navy photographer John Stringer said were not the ones he took of the brain, are consistent with a shot into the back of Kennedy's head.

Important questions obviously arise: Why did the military deem it necessary to conduct a second brain examination, one that the evidence indicates involved a brain that did not belong to Kennedy? What did the first examination of Kennedy's brain — the one that Stringer photographed — reveal? Why would the U.S. military engage in what would seem to be very nefarious conduct in the autopsy of a president of the United States?

We'll explore those questions later, but now, let's return to my articles "The Kennedy Casket Conspiracy" and "The Shot That Killed Kennedy" (both included as appendices in this book), and explore the secret, early delivery of the president's body to the Bethesda morgue in the context of the gunshot that hit Kennedy in the head. It will be convenient for the reader to read those two articles before my next chapter.

9

On the surface of things, the federal government's conduct with respect to the autopsy of President John F. Kennedy makes no sense at all. Indeed, much of how the government handled the aftermath of the assassination doesn't fit in with how we would ordinarily expect the government to react in such an extraordinary crisis.

Let's recap. Someone has just assassinated the president of the United States. Lee Harvey Oswald has been arrested as a prime suspect in the murder. The case against Oswald seems persuasive. He works in the building from which people heard shots being fired. A rifle supposedly belonging to him is found on the same floor on which he worked. A sniper's nest is also found there, along with shell casings from the rifle.

Such being the case, how would we expect law enforcement to react, especially when some federal official has just been murdered? Ordinarily, we would expect government at all levels to do two things: (1) do everything possible to marshal and preserve the evidence against the person they've arrested for the crime, and (2) conduct a massive investigation, leaving no stone unturned, into whether there were other people involved in the assassination.

Yet in the Kennedy assassination, the exact opposite was done in both respects. That simply makes no sense.

Let's consider some of the anomalies — the things that just don't fit together, with how we ordinarily would expect the government to react to this type of crisis.

Why would the government be so insistent on preventing the Dallas medical examiner from conducting the autopsy on the president's body? Why would the Secret Service be so intent on removing the body from the hospital and delivering it to Air Force One? The Secret Service was told that Texas law required the autopsy. The Secret Service also had to know that the autopsy report would play a critical role in the criminal prosecution of the person charged with the murder.

Why forcibly remove the body? Why brandish guns in the process? Why jeopardize the later criminal prosecution of the person charged with the murder? Why not, instead, cooperate with the Texas authorities? Why not work together to get the accused convicted of the crime?

After all, it's not as though the body was sitting in some foreign country, and it's not as though the autopsy would take weeks or months to conduct. The autopsy would be conducted in Texas and would take no more than three or four hours. The new president, Lyndon Johnson, could have immediately flown back to Washington, allowing Mrs. Kennedy to return a few hours later on Air Force Two with her husband's body.

Isn't that the way we would ordinarily expect the government to conduct itself?

Indeed, why would Johnson be sitting out on the tarmac in Air Force One, instead of immediately flying out of Dallas, especially since he, himself, had already raised the specter of a foreign attack on the United States? Wouldn't you expect him to get into the air immediately and return to Washington? Indeed, why would he take the time to change planes, from Air Force Two to Air Force One, and even the time to shift the luggage between the two planes? Why would he wait for a Dallas federal judge to drive to Love Field to swear him in as president? Does that make any sense at all, especially since nuclear missiles might be launched against the United States at any moment?

Why place the autopsy in the hands of the U.S. military? What in the world did the military have to do with it? This is ostensibly a civilian country, one that is run by civilians. The nation wasn't at war. The president was presumed to have been shot by a lone nut, not by some enemy nation-state with which the United States was at war. Why was it necessary to have the military conduct the autopsy rather than the Dallas civilian authorities or even a civilian medical examiner in Washington, D.C.?

Why was it necessary to remove the president's body from the Dallas casket and secretly deliver it into the Bethesda morgue at 6:30 p.m., more than an hour and a half before the formal autopsy began? Why was it necessary to deceive Mrs. Kennedy, the president's brother Robert Kennedy, and most of the rest of the world into thinking that the casket they were escorting from Andrews Air Force Base to Bethesda Naval Hospital had the president's body in it? Why was it necessary to engage in the secret body-shifting from casket to casket?

Why do the recollections of the Dallas physicians with respect to the wounds of the president differ so markedly from what the official autopsy photographs reveal? Why did the Dallas doctors distinctly remember a large hole in the back of Kennedy's head, indicating a shot from the front and an exit wound in the back of the head?

Why were the Dallas doctors insistent that the bullet hole in Kennedy's throat indicated a separate shot from the front when the autopsy report ultimately reflected that it was an exit wound from a shot to the back of the neck, from a bullet that seemed to have magical qualities? Indeed, how was it that the Bethesda autopsy physicians initially came up with a wound in the back of Kennedy's shoulder, which later evolved into a wound at the back of his neck?

Why were there unidentified people in suits at the autopsy giving orders as to how the autopsy should proceed and obstructing the proper conduct of the autopsy?

Why did the official autopsy photographer say that he didn't take photographs that are in the official autopsy records?

Why all the machinations with the so-called magic bullet?

Why did autopsy physician James Humes burn his notes and earlier drafts of the official autopsy report?

Why were there two separate brain examinations, the second one involving a brain that failed to reflect the massive damage to Kennedy's brain caused by the headshot that ended his life?

Why were the military autopsy personnel totally unconcerned with the possibility of having to testify about their findings in a criminal prosecution of the person charged with the offense? After all — don't forget the autopsy occurred while Oswald was still alive.

Why were autopsy personnel ordered to keep secret for the rest of their lives what they had witnessed during the autopsy? Why were they required to sign secrecy oaths, on pain of court-martial and severe punishment for violation? Why did the military years later resist releasing autopsy personnel from their oaths of secrecy?

Indeed, why did the government order most of its records in the Kennedy investigation, including the autopsy records, to be kept secret from the American people for 75 years? What national-security concern could possibly warrant that type of secrecy, especially given that the case simply involved, supposedly, just a lone nut who it was thought had assassinated the president?

Does that make any sense? There are just too many anomalies, too many questions, too many strange things, given the paradigm under which we are operating: that a lone nut assassinated Kennedy.

There is an alternative paradigm, however, one in which all the anomalies, all the mysterious occurrences, and all the weirdness disappear. It is a paradigm in which everything the government did becomes reasonable, rational, logical, and normal.

Let's examine that alternative paradigm.

Assume that soon after the assassination, the government's objective became to hide all evidence of conspiracy in the assassination of Kennedy. Assume that its aim was to place the entire responsibility for the murder on Lee Harvey Oswald.

For the time being, set aside any questions about why the government would do that. For now, just focus on the strict parameters of this alternative paradigm — that the government's aim was to hide any evidence of a conspiracy.

A major part of that objective would necessarily involve hiding any evidence of shots coming from the front of the president's motorcade. If even one shot was fired from the front, that would indicate that Oswald had at least one Confederate helping him with the assassination.

Thus, to achieve the objective under this alternative paradigm, the government would necessarily have to hide any evidence that shots had been fired from the front, e.g., from the grassy knoll in Dealey Plaza.

That would mean that taking control over the autopsy would be of critical importance. If the president had been shot from the front, the autopsy report and supporting photographs and X-rays would reveal that. Indeed, that's the purpose of an autopsy in a homicide case. It would thus be necessary to take control over the autopsy to ensure that such evidence would be suppressed.

Notice, now, that under this alternative paradigm, everything that before seemed strange and unusual now appears perfectly normal and natural.

The Secret Service knows that it has to get the president's body out of the hands of the Dallas medical examiner to prevent him from performing an honest autopsy. The matter is so important that the Secret Service uses force, even implicitly threatening the use of deadly force, to get the body out of Parkland Hospital and delivered to Air Force One.

It now makes sense that Johnson would wait for the body, to eliminate the possibility that something could go wrong, such as Texas law-enforcement agents stopping the ambulance that was transporting the president's body to Love Field and preventing it from being removed from the state before the legally required autopsy had been performed. If things went wrong, Johnson would still be there in Dallas to make some emergency calls to clear things up, perhaps to the Dallas County district attorney or to other officials with whom he was friends.

It also now makes sense that Johnson would deliver the body into the hands of the military. The military could be ordered to do whatever was necessary to hide evidence of shots from the front during the autopsy. The entire matter could be classified as top-secret. Military personnel could be relied on to keep classified matters secret, especially when ordered to do so and after signing an express secrecy oath.

It now makes sense that the president's body would be secretly removed from the Dallas casket, placed into the cheap shipping casket, and delivered into the morgue more than an hour and a half before the formal autopsy finally began. The autopsy physicians would have needed the time to make a careful pre-autopsy inspection of the body and to make any necessary alterations to the body in preparation for the autopsy.

Under our alternative paradigm, it now makes sense that there would have been unidentified experts at the autopsy supervising and monitoring it to ensure that everything needed to cover up shots from the front would be conducted properly, including falsification of the wounds, the photographs, and the X-rays.

The machinations with the magic bullet now make sense, given the need to match the number of shots fired with the maximum number of shots that Oswald could have fired.

As Douglas Horne details in *Inside the Assassination Records Review Board*, and as author David Lifton theorized in 1981 in his book *Best Evidence*, there is substantial evidence that the autopsy physicians engaged in pre-autopsy surgery to obscure evidence of shots from the front, something that would normally be considered extraordinarily unusual, but not under our alternative paradigm.

Recall that the Dallas physicians had observed a big hole at the back of Kennedy's head, a hole that would indicate an exit wound, meaning that a shot came from the front. Recall also that the official autopsy photos show the back of Kennedy's head to be intact.

So where do government officials say the bullet entered and exited? Their position is that Oswald, the supposed lone-nut assassin, fired a bullet that hit Kennedy in the back of the head and exited from the top of the head, producing a massive exit wound on the top of Kennedy's head.

Where was the entry point exactly under the government's version? Well, that's a good question. The autopsy doctors could never get their stories straight on that. At one point they said that it was near the bottom of the back of the head, which obviously would create problems for a bullet that was supposed to have exited from the top of the head. So their later version, one adopted long after the body had been buried, was that the entry hole was actually several inches higher on the head.

By the same token, the Dallas physicians had not observed the large wound that encompassed much of the top of Kennedy's head, which government officials maintained was the real exit wound, one that reflected a shot from the back. How is that possible? Why wouldn't treating physicians at one of the finest trauma centers in the country have seen a giant exit wound on the top of the president's head?

The answer might well lie in pre-autopsy surgery that altered the condition of the body. Consider, for example, this excerpt from the official report of the two FBI agents who attended the autopsy, Francis X. O'Neill, Jr. and James W. Sibert, which is what caused Lifton to begin exploring the possibility of pre-autopsy surgery:

> Following the removal of the wrapping, it was ascertained that the Presidents clothing had been removed and it was also apparent that a tracheotomy had been performed, as well as surgery of the head area, namely, in the top of the skull.

Ordinarily, pre-autopsy surgery would be considered bizarre. Under our alternative paradigm, however — a paradigm under which the government aims to hide any evidence of a shot from the front — such pre-autopsy surgery would be perfectly normal and rational, given the government's aim of obscuring evidence of shots from the front and producing evidence of shots from the back.

The obvious question arises: Why would the government do all that? Why would federal officials engage in a plan to cover up evidence of a conspiracy in the assassination of President Kennedy? Why would orders be given to the U.S. military to falsify the autopsy results on the president's body in an attempt to hide any evidence of shots fired from the front? Why would military personnel follow such orders and swear on their oath to never reveal what they had done?

The answer lies in the two most important words in the lives of the American people in our lifetime: national security. We'll examine how in the next chapter.

10

Suppose that on the flight back from Dallas on November 22, 1963, President Johnson made the following telephone call to the two military pathologists who would be conducting the autopsy on President Kennedy's body, Navy commanders James Humes and J. Thornton Boswell:

> Gentlemen, this is the president speaking. Our nation finds itself in a grave emergency, one involving the greatest threat to national security in our nation's history. As you know, President Kennedy has just been shot and killed.
>
> The assassin, a man named Lee Harvey Oswald, has been taken into custody. CIA Director Helms has informed me that the man is a communist. He is a former U.S. Marine who rejected his country, moved to the Soviet Union, and attempted to defect. In the process, he gave top-secret, classified information to the Soviets, information that he acquired while stationed at the Atsugi Naval Air Facility in Japan, where our U2 spy planes were based. Don't ask me why he wasn't charged with treason on his return to the United States. We'll deal with that later when he's prosecuted for murdering President Kennedy.
>
> The problem is that Oswald did not operate alone. Shots were also fired from the front of the motorcade, with one shot hitting the president in the throat and another hitting him in front of the head and exiting the rear. This has been confirmed by President Kennedy's personal physician, Navy Admiral George Burkley, who was present in the president's emergency room at Parkland. We also have the statement of a Dallas police officer who encountered a man flashing a Secret Service badge in the area from which the frontal shots were fired. We have confirmed that there were no Secret Service agents in that area.
>
> Director Helms informs me that as recently as two months ago, Oswald was engaged in pro-Castro activities in New Orleans. More ominously, the CIA has photographic and audiotape evidence establishing that one month ago, Oswald traveled to Mexico City, where he visited both the

Cuban and Soviet embassies. At the latter, he met with a known Soviet assassin, a man named Valery Kostikov.

I am sure you understand the implications of all this but let me make them clear: our country is once again faced with the imminent prospect of nuclear war, and the danger is even more real than it was 13 months ago during the Cuban Missile Crisis. Given the evidence, there is only one reasonable possibility: Oswald and his confederates were acting on behalf of Cuba and the Soviet Union.

I don't need to tell you that this assassination is an act of war, an attack by the communists on our president and our country. Ordinarily, I would be ordering an immediate mobilization of the U.S. armed forces in preparation for retaliation by the United States, beginning with a military invasion of Cuba.

However, Director Helms has also provided me with extremely disquieting information. It turns out that President Kennedy and his brother Robert, the attorney general, have been operating a damned Murder, Inc., in the Caribbean, involving repeated assassination attempts by the CIA on Castro. Even worse, Helms informs me that the CIA had a full-fledged assassination partnership with the Mafia to assassinate Castro, with the full approval of the Kennedy brothers. Yes, the Mafia.

Under these circumstances, I have decided that I cannot take our nation to war, a nuclear war that would inevitably kill tens of millions of Americans and countless more people around the world. How could I wreak so much death and destruction knowing that we were the ones who started this assassination business and that Castro and the Soviets were simply retaliating?

I need your help to prevent such a war from breaking out. Having removed the president's body from Dallas to prevent the Dallas authorities from conducting an autopsy, we are now returning the body to Washington so that our military will have control over the autopsy.

I am hereby ordering you, on the basis of national security, to do whatever is necessary to hide any evidence of shots having been fired from the front. We need to pin this thing solely on that no-good, dirty communist traitor Oswald. We need to do whatever is necessary to prevent mushroom clouds from rising above American cities.

I don't need to tell you the importance of secrecy here. If the American people were to discover that their beloved president has been killed by Castro and Khrushchev, the pressure for retaliation would be insurmountable.

Therefore, I am hereby ordering you to never, ever disclose what you are about to do to anyone, including any investigative body.

I fully understand that I am ordering you to do some unsavory and unpleasant things, but as you can see, they are absolutely essential to national security. I take full responsibility for your actions, and if they are ever uncovered, I will issue an immediate presidential pardon to everyone who followed my orders.

What you are about to do must be taken to the grave with you. Your role in saving our country and the world from nuclear war will never be acknowledged. But one of these days you will be able to go to your deathbeds knowing that you played a critical role in saving the lives of tens of millions of innocent people, including perhaps your own families, from an illegitimate and ill-founded nuclear war.

There will be a CIA officer present at the autopsy. He is a trained pathologist. He is in charge. He will be standing in my stead, as your commander-in-chief. You are to follow his orders during the autopsy.

One more thing, gentlemen: I need your solemn, sworn oath as military officers that you will never, ever disclose this conversation and what you are about to do to anyone for any reason, including congressional hearings and investigative bodies. Thank you for your service to our country, and God bless America.

Given such a grave threat to national security on November 22, 1963, there is no way that any military officer would have refused to follow the orders of his commander-in-chief. Once the president explained the nature of the emergency — and the very real threat to national security with the very real prospect of nuclear war between the United States and the Soviet Union — every single military officer in the country would have faithfully followed whatever orders were issued to him by the president, especially if by doing so the officer would have been helping to save his country from a wrongfully instigated nuclear war. And having sworn on his oath to take such highly classified information to his grave, he would have done so.

The circumstantial evidence indicates that the national-security/nuclear-war rationale was being employed in the aftermath of the assassination at the same time that determined efforts were being made to immediately shut down the investigation and pin the assassination solely on Oswald.

When Chief Justice of the United States Earl Warren refused Johnson's invitation to serve on what later became known as the Warren Commission, based on the impropriety of a Supreme Court justice serving on an executive-branch panel, Johnson persuaded him to change his mind by referring to the possibility of a nuclear war that would kill some millions of Americans. Consider this excerpt from the page entitled "Walkthrough: Formation of the Warren Commission" on the Mary Ferrell Foundation website, a site dedicated to exploring the Kennedy assassination:

Nov 29, 8:55 p.m. Phone call between President Johnson and Richard Russell
In this fascinating call, the last of the day, Johnson tells Russell that he has named him to the Commission over Russell's objections, because you've got to lend your name to this thing and because "we've got to take this out of the arena where they're testifying that Khrushchev and Castro did this and did that and kicking us into a war that can kill 40 million Americans in an hour...." LBJ also tells Russell the story of how Warren turned him down repeatedly until Johnson "pulled out what Hoover told me about a little incident in Mexico City."

Consider the following excerpt on the same website page:

Nov 24, 4:00 p.m. Account of phone call between FBI Director Hoover and White House Aide Walter Jenkins
Hoover began by reporting "There is nothing further on the Oswald case except that he is dead." At the end of the call, Hoover noted the need to have "something issued so we can convince the public that Oswald is the real assassin," and that (Assistant Attorney General) "Katzenbach thinks that the President might appoint a Presidential Commission of three outstanding citizens to make a determination."

Consider this excerpt from the same website page regarding a memo issued by Deputy U.S. Attorney General Nicholas Katzenbach issued just 3 days after the assassination:

Nov 25, time unknown Katzenbach Memo
Titled "Memorandum for Mr. Moyers," Katzenbach lays out the need for a public statement on the assassination. Katzenbach states that the public must be satisfied that Oswald was the assassin; that he did not have

confederates who are still at large; and that the evidence was such that he would have been convicted at trial.

On page 1507 of volume 5 of *Inside the Assassination Records Review Board* author Douglas Horne recounts a fascinating incident that indicates that Robert Kennedy had been provided with the national-security/nuclear-war scenario:

> In the days immediately following President Kennedy's assassination, the Kennedy family — reportedly the late President's brother — Bobby sent an unofficial emissary to the Soviet Union to inform its leadership, via the KGB, that in spite of the fact that the accused assassin had been a defector to the Soviet Union, and apparently had emotional and ideological ties to Castro's Cuba, the Kennedy family did not believe that the USSR had anything to do with the assassination, but instead was convinced that JFK's murder was the result of a large, right-wing domestic political conspiracy.

Under this national-security/nuclear-war paradigm, then, the pieces of the JFK assassination seem to fall into place. What appear to be anomalies and strange actions, especially during Kennedy's autopsy, become reasonable and rational. Shots are purportedly fired from both the front and the back. The authorities take into custody the purported shooter from the back, Lee Harvey Oswald. Given Oswald's pro-Cuba sympathies and connections to the Soviet Union (e.g., his attempted defection to the Soviet Union, his recent pro-Castro activities in New Orleans, and his recent visits to the Cuban and Soviet embassies in Mexico City), the only reasonable conclusion that can be drawn is that Oswald and the shooter in the front were operating as agents of Cuba and the Soviet Union, which would almost certainly mean nuclear war between the United States and the Soviet Union.

Since Kennedy's assassination, however, would have been retaliatory in nature, given Kennedy's repeated attempts to assassinate Castro, it would have been reasonable for Johnson to do what was necessary to hide the conspiracy from the American people and to pin the assassination entirely on Oswald, in order to avoid nuclear war. Johnson would have ordered the Secret Service to take control of Kennedy's body at Parkland and put it in the hands of the military, which could then be relied upon to loyally follow orders based on national security by doing whatever was necessary to conceal evidence of shots fired from the front during the autopsy. It would then be logical to keep matters relating to the autopsy and, for that matter, matters relating to the later Warren Commission investigation into the assassination, secret from the American people for 75 years.

If this is what actually happened — if President Kennedy was hit by shots fired from the front, and if the aim of President Johnson and other high officials of the national-security state was to conceal the evidence of such shots in order to avoid an illegitimate nuclear war, wouldn't this mean then that we should be as grateful to Johnson for avoiding a nuclear war as we are to President Kennedy for avoiding nuclear war during the Cuban Missile Crisis thirteen months before? Wouldn't this mean that we should be grateful to the national-security establishment, especially those military officials who conducted the Kennedy autopsy, for doing what was necessary to protect us in what arguably was the biggest national-security crisis in our nation's history?

Well, not exactly, because, you see, there is a fatal flaw in this scenario, a critically important one that we will examine in the next chapter.

11

In the previous chapter, we examined a paradigm in which the government's aim was to conceal evidence of shots that hit President Kennedy from the front and to create the appearance that all shots came from the back, i.e., from Lee Harvey Oswald.

Why would the government do that?

Because the evidence pointed to a Cuban-Soviet assassination of Kennedy, given Oswald's sympathies for Cuba and Fidel Castro and his connections to the Soviet Union, and given that shots were fired from both the front and the back.

Under that paradigm, Lyndon Johnson decided that he could not in good conscience take the retaliatory steps that would almost certainly lead to an all-out nuclear war between the superpowers, for the CIA, along with the Mafia, had begun the assassination war against Castro with repeated efforts to assassinate him during the Kennedy administration.

Therefore, Johnson, on grounds of national security, ordered the Secret Service to take control of the president's body at Parkland and deliver it to Air Force One for transportation back to Washington, whereupon he ordered military personnel at Bethesda Naval Hospital, again on grounds of national security, to conceal evidence of shots from the front and to make it appear as though all the shots came from the rear.

Within this paradigm, the anomalies and unusual circumstances surrounding the investigation into Kennedy's assassination and the subsequent autopsy disintegrate. The government's strange conduct during the autopsy and the government's quick conclusion that Oswald was a lone-nut assassin now become logical and rational, in that they were considered necessary to spare America and the world from an illegitimate nuclear war that would kill countless millions of people in the United States, the Soviet Union, Cuba, and elsewhere around the world.

However, as well as the pieces of the puzzle fit under this paradigm, it has a fatal flaw in it and, therefore, must be discarded, at least in part, and replaced with another paradigm, one in which everything once again fits together and has no fatal flaw to it.

Consider the following timeline:

1:50 p.m. — Oswald is arrested at the Texas Theater.

Shortly after 2:00 p.m. — The casket departs Parkland Hospital for Love Field, where it is loaded onto Air Force One at 2:15 p.m.

Do you see the problem?

In Chapter 1, I described the amazing encounter between the Secret Service and the Dallas County medical examiner at Parkland Hospital. Led by Secret Service agent Roy Kellerman, the Secret Service agents at Parkland refused to permit the medical examiner to conduct the autopsy on the body and insisted on removing it from the hospital so that it could be delivered to Love Field, where Johnson was waiting for it.

Even though the medical examiner told Kellerman that Texas law required the autopsy to be conducted in Texas, Kellerman and his men, screaming and yelling and employing profanities and, most amazingly, opening their coats to expose their guns, forcibly overcame the medical examiner's resistance, and transported the casket to an ambulance, which carried the casket to Love Field, where Johnson's people had removed some seats in the rear of Air Force One to make room for it. The casket was loaded onto the plane and taken to Andrews Air Force Base, where it was transported to Bethesda Naval Hospital, albeit without Kennedy's body in it.

Do you see the fatal flaw now?

First of all, consider once again that that is not how we would ordinarily expect the Secret Service to act. Wouldn't we instead expect the Secret Service to comply with the law and also to cooperate with local officials to help get the person or persons responsible for the murder convicted and punished? They had to know that the criminal prosecution of people ultimately charged with the crime would necessarily turn, at least in part, on the autopsy report. Why violate the law? Why threaten to use force against medical personnel who had just tried to save the president's life? Why jeopardize the criminal prosecution of whoever was later charged with the crime?

There is only one reasonable explanation for the Secret Service's conduct. They had been ordered to get the casket out of that hospital, come hell or high water. There is no way that they would engage in such extraordinary conduct without having been ordered to do so. The only person who would have had the moral authority to issue such an extraordinary order was the man who was waiting at Love Field for the casket — the man whose personnel were already removing seats from the back of his plane to accommodate the casket.

That man was Lyndon Johnson. There is just no other reasonable explanation for the Secret Service's extraordinary conduct at Parkland Hospital.

If the Secret Service's conduct in the removal of the casket from Parkland Hospital was all there was to the situation, one might say, oh well, people sometimes do dumb things in a crisis, and let it go.

But not here, and not given the extraordinary measures that later surrounded the autopsy, as detailed in this book. In retrospect, it is clear that the Secret Service's conduct in forcibly removing Kennedy's casket from Parkland Hospital and delivering it to Johnson's plane was the first step in the process of getting the autopsy under the control of the military in order to conceal the evidence that shots had been fired from the front.

Do you see the problem now?

Under the paradigm we are considering, the decision to conceal evidence of shots from the front necessarily depended on having a communist in custody. Thus, the problem is that when the first step of this national-security plan to protect America from an illegitimate nuclear war was implemented, there was no communist in custody yet. Or more precisely, there had not been enough time to ascertain Oswald's connection to Cuba and the Soviet Union and to think about what to do about it before implementing a national-security plan to suppress evidence that shots had been fired from the front.

That's the fatal flaw. Johnson implemented his national-security plan too soon. He implemented it before there was a national-security problem that was later used to justify the plan.

Consider, once again, the timeline:

1:50 p.m. — Oswald is arrested at the Texas Theater.

Shortly after 2:00 p.m. — The casket departs Parkland Hospital for Love Field, where it is loaded onto Air Force One at 2:15 p.m.

Since the casket departed Parkland Hospital shortly after 2 p.m., that means that the altercation between the Secret Service and the Dallas medical examiner occurred at, say, 1:55 p.m.

Five minutes (1:50 p.m. versus 1:55 p.m.) is obviously not enough time to take Oswald to the police station, have the FBI and CIA establish his communist background, including his recent trips to Mexico City, deliver the information to Johnson, have Johnson ponder and deliberate over the consequences, and then have Johnson decide to implement a plan, based on national security, to have the military take control over the autopsy in order to suppress evidence of shots fired from the front.

If Oswald had been killed at the School Book Depository, say at 12:45, then that would have provided a respectable period of time of 1 hour — to do all that. But he wasn't killed at the School Book Depository. He departed the building and wasn't captured until 1:50 p.m., which was about the same time that the Secret Service was implementing the first step in a national-security plan that had no communists with ties to Cuba and the Soviet Union in hand to justify the implementation of the national-security plan.

At this point, the reader might note that Kellerman, the Secret Service agent who led the contingent of Secret Service agents who forcibly removed the casket from Parkland Hospital, was also the Secret Service agent in the front passenger seat of the president's car during the Dallas motorcade. He was also one of the two Secret Service agents (the other being William Greer, the driver of Kennedy's car in the Dallas motorcade) who were involved in the middle casket switch that took place before the start of the formal autopsy at the Bethesda morgue.

So where does that now leave us?

It leaves us with the Secret Service implementing the first step in a national-security plan to suppress evidence that shots had been fired from the front of Kennedy's motorcade without having the communist on which the plan turned in custody long enough to justify the plan.

When he was at Parkland, waiting to ascertain Kennedy's condition, Johnson raised the prospect that the assassination might be part of a Soviet attack on the United States. After Kennedy died, Johnson stated at Parkland, "I think I had better get out of here ... before you announce it. We don't know whether this is a worldwide conspiracy, whether they are after me as well as they were after President Kennedy...."

Johnson's actions, however, belie any concern for the real possibility of a potential attack from the Soviet Union.

For one thing, he waited at the hospital some 40 minutes until Kennedy had been declared dead. Would Johnson have sat around waiting at the hospital if he honestly believed that the Soviets might be launching nuclear missiles at the United States? Not on your life.

Then, once he departed the hospital and got to Love Field, he decided to take the time to transfer from Air Force Two to Air Force One, including having his luggage transferred from Air Force Two to Air Force One. The planes were duplicates and they were both returning to Washington.

Then the personnel on Air Force One began removing seats from the back of the plane to accommodate Kennedy's casket, which they were waiting for. Getting the casket onboard was obviously of greater importance to Johnson than the possibility of a nuclear attack from the Soviet Union.

Then Johnson waited for a federal judge to arrive to swear him in before he finally took off at 2:38CST — more than two hours after Kennedy had been assassinated.

Does that look like a man who was terribly concerned about the possibility that the assassination of Kennedy might well be the first step in a Soviet attack on the United States? Or does it look like a man who was certain that the Soviets had nothing to do with the assassination and who knew that his national-security rationale for taking the body out of Parkland and delivering it into the hands of the military at Bethesda Naval Hospital was bogus?

Let's now examine another paradigm, this one also based on national security, a paradigm in which the pieces to the Kennedy assassination puzzle will, once again, fall into logical and rational place, but this time with no fatal flaw to it. We'll do that in the final chapter of this book.

12

Under the national-security paradigm that we examined in Chapter 11, Lyndon Johnson and the national-security establishment knew that the surefire way to shut down an investigation into the assassination was to employ the two most important words in the lives of the American people in our lifetime — "national security." Those two words, along with the almost-certain prospect of a nuclear war, were guaranteed to secure cooperation in the cover-up by everyone within the circles of power. Citing national security also guaranteed that a hush of silent and trusting acquiescence would sweep across America when a shroud of secrecy was placed over an official investigation into an assassination of a U.S. president supposedly committed by a lone nut.

Let's now overlay a new paradigm on our situation, one that is also based on national security — a paradigm in which shots are intentionally fired at the president from the front, while the supposed shooter is in the rear, for the express purpose of ensuring a national-security shutdown of any investigation into the assassination and a willingness to cooperate with a subsequent cover-up, especially with the autopsy.

Douglas Horne summed up the tenets of this national-security paradigm in this excerpt from *Inside the Assassination Records Review Board*:

> It is an inconvenient truth that President Kennedy was essentially at war with the conservative establishment — the power elites if you will — within both the American intelligence community and the American military ... that his Vice President, perhaps the most unscrupulous, power-hungry, and corrupt politician ever to come out of the state of Texas, was placed on the ticket by JFK in 1960 as a result of blackmail ... that JFK planned to drop Lyndon Johnson from the Democratic ticket in 1964, and replace him with a different Vice Presidential running mate ... that the investigations of the two major scandals that were chasing LBJ in 1963 were immediately quashed following his assumption of the Presidency, but that is the case.

It is an inconvenient truth that if JFK had still been alive in January 1965 — whether he had won the 1964 Presidential election or not — that J. Edgar Hoover would have been forced to step down on the mandatory retirement age on New Year's Day, 1965 ... that the new President, LBJ, waived the mandatory retirement age for Hoover — something Kennedy did not intend to do — one week before Hoover testified before the Warren Commission and blamed the assassination of JFK on a lone nut, but that was the case.

It is an inconvenient truth that the planned U.S. withdrawal from Vietnam directed by President Kennedy, and being implemented by his Secretary of Defense, Robert McNamara, was almost immediately reversed after the assassination by LBJ and that same Robert McNamara ... that the arms control agreements and détente with the Soviet Union that President Kennedy had planned on pursuing after the Nuclear Test Ban Treaty never came about, but instead were replaced by a massive nuclear arms race, but that is the case.

It is an inconvenient truth that the Kennedy family sent a secret emissary to the Soviet Union immediately after JFK's death to tell the Soviet leadership that they knew the Soviet Union was not involved in the assassination, and that they believed that JFK had been assassinated by a right-wing domestic conspiracy ... that the KGB *secretly* instructed the staff of its Residency in New York City in September of 1965 that President Lyndon Johnson was responsible for the assassination of President John F. Kennedy, but that is the case.

It is an inconvenient truth that President Kennedy's poor health, progressive foreign policy, and his reckless addiction to promiscuous sex — his alleged immorality — were probably used as leverage to recruit insiders with the Secret Service White House Detail to assist with "security stripping" during the Dallas leg of his Texas trip, as well as with the subsequent coverup of the assassination ... that President Kennedy's two closest personal aides, Kenneth O'Donnell and Dave Powers, both withheld from the Warren Commission that they heard shots emanate from the grassy knoll in Dealey Plaza, *because the FBI asked them not to say it*, but that is the case.

It is an inconvenient truth that there is scientific evidence indicating that Lee Harvey Oswald shot *no one* on November 22, 1963 ... that both the "magic bullet" and the two bullet fragments found in the front seat of the

Presidential limousine appear to have been *planted evidence* designed to implicate Oswald, but that is the case....

It is an inconvenient truth that JFK's assassination and the ensuing coverup were "an inside job," but how can an open-minded person who has studied the evidence in the Kennedy assassination conclude otherwise? Missing autopsy photographs, missing autopsy x-rays, forged skull x-rays, fraudulent autopsy photographs that misrepresent wounds and conceal (rather than reveal) the actual damage, a missing brain, two brain exams, dishonest photographs of a substituted brain, a rewritten autopsy report, missing skull bone fragments, seized videotapes of the hospital press conference about the President's death, security stripping of the Dallas motorcade, a Presidential Commission and an FBI that both pointedly ignored overwhelming eyewitness and earwitness testimony of shots from multiple directions, planted bullets that ballistically "match" the assassination weapon, an interrupted chain of custody on the President's body, altered wound on the President's body, and the alteration and suppression of a shocking motion picture film of the assassination, *all lead to the inescapable conclusion that the assassination of John F. Kennedy was an inside job.*

No, it does not make us feel good to acknowledge this — but it is the only way to regain our self-respect as a people.

The uncertain or skeptical reader will hopefully obtain a better feel for the existence of the cabal that removed President Kennedy from office, and the motivations driving its different elements, as I explore in this final chapter the overwhelming evidence that it was the national-security establishment — and by this I mean the power elites that really ran this country in 1963 — that got rid of President Kennedy, not just a few rogue elephants. In every true sense of the word, the assassination of President Kennedy was a coup d'etat, but it was a coup "by consensus," not the isolated act of two or three unprincipled individuals. Lyndon B. Johnson and J. Edgar Hoover were simply the principal 'enablers' of the plot; its genesis and growing motivation was found in the strong opposition of the conservative power elites in the United States to JFK's foreign policy, which they believed strongly threatened both their interests, and the future survival of the nation....

(Horne, volume 5, pages 1470–1471; emphasis in original).

During the 1970s the official investigation into the Kennedy assassination was reopened by the House Select Committee on Assassinations (HSCA), owing to widespread public skepticism surrounding the Warren Commission Report. The attorney who was selected to lead the investigation was Richard Sprague, a brilliant, fiercely independent, and honest prosecutor from Philadelphia, who was assisted by an attorney of equally high caliber, Robert K. Tanenbaum.

In his new book *Last Word: My Indictment of the CIA in the Murder of JFK*, which includes an introduction by Tanenbaum, attorney Mark Lane explains what then happened (Lane, pages 217–223).

Before Sprague was able to launch his investigation, the CIA insisted on his signing a secrecy agreement in which Sprague would vow to never reveal anything he learned from the CIA during the course of the investigation. Sprague refused to sign the agreement, given his ethical obligation to go wherever the investigation might lead him, including the possibility of having to make the CIA a target of the investigation.

Immediately, a campaign to oust Sprague was launched in Congress, creating a political furor in which Congress refused to fund Sprague's investigation. Unable to proceed, both Sprague and Tanenbaum resigned, being replaced by a man named Robert Blakey.

Blakey ended up signing the CIA's secrecy oath. At the end of the investigation, the HSCA concluded that shots had, in fact, been fired at Kennedy from the front but intimated that the conspiracy to kill the president involved the Mafia.

There was at least one big problem, however, with that intimation: The Mafia had absolutely nothing to do with the autopsy of President John F. Kennedy. The autopsy was controlled entirely by the U.S. national-security state, specifically the U.S. military.

Obviously, the Warren Commission never seriously considered the possibility that the CIA had engineered Kennedy's assassination, for three reasons:

First, sitting as a member of the Warren Commission (and appointed by President Johnson) was Alan Dulles, the former director of the CIA whom Kennedy had fired after the Bay of Pigs disaster. There was no possibility that the CIA would be made a target of investigation so long as its former director was serving on the commission.

Second, the circumstantial evidence indicates that the Warren Commission was fed the national-security, nuclear war rationale (as set forth in Chapters 10 and 11 of this book) that was used to immediately shut down the investigation and pin the assassination solely on Oswald.

Third, the Warren Commission was composed entirely of mainstream establishment figures who would have considered it inconceivable that such a regime-change operation could have been effected in the United States.

In other words, people could accept that the U.S. national-security state would go abroad with brilliant, even ingenious, plots to oust the prime ministers or presidents of other countries who threatened U.S. national security (e.g., Iran, Guatemala, Vietnam, and Cuba), but it was simply considered inconceivable that it would ever effect a regime-change operation domestically to protect America from a president whose supposed naïveté, inexperience, and bumbling was threatening national security at home at the height of the Cold War.

Ironically, however, when he was alive, Kennedy himself considered such a scenario conceivable. Horne quotes Kennedy telling his friend Paul "Red" Fay, undersecretary of the Navy, the following:

> It's possible. It could happen in this country, but the conditions would have to be just right. If, for example, the country had a young President, and he had a Bay of Pigs, there would be a certain uneasiness. Maybe the military would do a little criticizing behind his back, but this would be written off as the usual military dissatisfaction with civilian control. Then if there were another Bay of Pigs, the reaction of the country would be, "Is he too young and inexperienced?" The military would almost feel that it was their patriotic obligation to stand ready to preserve the integrity of the nation, and only God knows just what segment of democracy they would be defending if they overthrew the elected establishment ... then, if there were a third Bay of Pigs, it could happen ... but it won't happen on my watch (Horne, volume 5, pages 1501–1502).

We must also bear in mind the prime directive of the national-security state: to protect our nation's national security and that they have all taken an oath to defend America from all enemies, both foreign and domestic. To this day, there are people who defend the CIA-supported coups in Guatemala (1954) and Chile (1973) by arguing that a constitution is not a suicide pact — that if the regime-change operations in those countries had not occurred, both nations would have definitely fallen to the communists.

Moreover, even today — almost 50 years after the assassination, the CIA steadfastly refuses to open all its files relating to the Kennedy assassination to the American people. As former *Washington Post* reporter and current Salon.com editor Jefferson Morley stated in a November 22, 2011, article entitled "The Holy Grail of the JFK Story":

> In 2003 I sued the CIA for the records of George Joannides, a secondary character in the JFK story. Eight years later, the Agency is still fighting the release of some 330 records on him, a legal defense that the New York Times aptly described in 2009 as "cagey." Agency lawyers are scheduled to appear in federal court later this year to argue that none of this antique material can be made public in any form — supposedly for reasons of "national security."

There you have them again, the two words that have played the most important role in the lives of the American people in our lifetime: national security!

In a 2009 *New York Times* article entitled "C.I.A. Is Still Cagey About Oswald Mystery" about the CIA's continued refusal to open its records on Joannides to the American people, Minnesota federal judge John R. Tunheim, who served as chairman of the Assassination Records Review Board, referred to the CIA's deception of the ARRB regarding Joannides' role in the Kennedy assassination investigation: "I think we were misled by the agency. This material should be released."

Even Robert Blakey, who replaced Sprague at the House Select Committee on Assassinations, later accused the CIA of obstruction of justice regarding Joannides. "I now believe the process lacked integrity precisely because of Joannides," he told PBS.

Several questions naturally arise: Was Kennedy's foreign policy, including his secret overtures to the Soviet Union and Cuba at the height of the Cold War, endangering America's national security? Did the national-security establishment construe Kennedy's foreign policy to be a threat to national security? Did the national-security state act to protect our nation's national security with a regime-change operation on November 22, 1963? Was national security used to shut down the investigation into the assassination, including through concealment of shots fired from the front by the military-controlled autopsy of the president's body? Has the

CIA engaged in deception, and does it still refuse to disclose information for reasons of national security or some other reason?

Some would say that the Kennedy assassination is irrelevant, given the long passage of time and the fact that all the actors in the assassination are probably dead.

I hold otherwise. I say that America made a grave mistake at the end of World War II in overlaying our constitutional republic with a national-security state. At the end of the war, America should have come home, brought all the troops home, and demobilized. The CIA should never have been established. The United States should never have adopted a Soviet-style system in order to fight a Cold War against the Soviet Union.

At the end of his term, President Eisenhower obviously started to recognize the danger of the military-industrial complex to American democracy. That's what his farewell address was all about — warning the American people of the monster that the military-industrial complex was becoming.

He wasn't the only one. A month after Kennedy's assassination, the *Washington Post* published an op-ed by former President Truman stating that the CIA had become a sinister force in American life. Truman's timing, while America was still grieving Kennedy's death, could not have been a coincidence.

Adopting the national-security state to wage a Cold War against the Soviet Union ended up changing America — for the worse, to the point where our nation now openly embraces such Soviet-like actions as assassination, torture, Gulags, arbitrary arrests, indefinite military detention, kangaroo tribunals, and support of foreign dictatorships.

The Cold War is over. It's time for America to restore its status as a constitutional republic. It's time to dismantle the national-security state.

What better way to honor the foreign-policy legacy of President John F. Kennedy?

A   The Kennedy Casket Conspiracy

Last November, a new book entitled *The Kennedy Detail: JFK's Secret Service Agents Break Their Silence*, by Gerald Blaine and Lisa McCubbin, promised to "reveal the inside story of the assassination, the weeks and days that led to it and its heartrending aftermath."

Unfortunately, however, while providing details of the events leading up to the assassination, the assassination itself, and President Kennedy's funeral, the book provided hardly any information on one of the most mysterious aspects of the assassination: what happened when Kennedy's body was delivered to the morgue at Bethesda Naval Hospital on the evening of the assassination.

For almost 50 years, people have debated the Kennedy assassination. Some claim that the Warren Commission got it right — that Kennedy was assassinated by Lee Harvey Oswald, a lone-nut assassin. Others contend that Kennedy was killed as part of a conspiracy.

It is not the purpose of this article to engage in that debate. The purpose of this article is simply to focus on what happened at Bethesda Naval Hospital on the evening of November 22, 1963, and, specifically, the events that took place prior to Kennedy's autopsy. What happened that night is so unusual that it cries out for a truthful explanation even after 47 years.

U.S. officials have long maintained that Kennedy's body was delivered to the Bethesda morgue in the heavy, ornamental, bronze casket in which the body had been placed at Parkland Hospital in Dallas.

The problem, however, is that the evidence establishes that Kennedy's body was actually delivered to the Bethesda morgue twice, at separate times and in separate caskets.

How does one resolve this problem? One option, obviously, is just to forget about it, given that the assassination took place almost a half-century ago. But it seems to me that since the matter is so unusual and since it involves a president of the United States, the American people — regardless of which side of the divide they fall on — lone-nut assassin or conspiracy — are entitled to a truthful explanation of what happened that night at

Bethesda. And the only ones who can provide it are U.S. officials, especially those in the Secret Service, the FBI, and the U.S. military, the agencies that were in control of events at Bethesda that night.

The facts of the casket controversy are set forth in detail in a five-volume work that was published in 2009 entitled *Inside the Assassination Records Review Board: The U.S. Government's Final Attempt to Reconcile the Conflicting Medical Evidence in the Assassination of JFK*. The author is Douglas P. Horne, who served as chief analyst for military records for the Assassination Records Review Board. The ARRB was the official board established to administer the JFK Records Act, which required federal departments and agencies to divulge to the public their files and records relating to the Kennedy assassination. The act was enacted after Oliver Stone's 1991 movie, *JFK*, produced a firestorm of public outcry against the U.S. government's decision to keep assassination-related records secret from the public for 75 years after the publication of the Warren Commission Report in 1964, and for 50 years after the publication of the House Select Committee on Assassinations Report in 1979.

Horne's book posits that high officials in the national-security state — i.e., the CIA, FBI, Secret Service, and U.S. military — planned and executed the assassination of John F. Kennedy and that the man who replaced Kennedy as president, Lyndon B. Johnson, orchestrated a cover-up of the conspiracy by telling officials that national security (i.e., a potential nuclear war, citing Oswald's activities relating to the Soviet Union and Cuba) necessitated shutting down an investigation into determining whether Kennedy's murder involved a conspiracy. Horne's book focuses primarily on the events surrounding the autopsy of Kennedy's body on the night of the assassination. As he, himself, acknowledges, his book expands upon the thesis set forth in a book published in 1981, entitled *Best Evidence* by David Lifton, which was nominated for a Pulitzer Prize and reached Number 4 on the *New York Times* best-seller list.

It was Lifton who originally challenged the official story that Kennedy's body was delivered only once to the Bethesda morgue. It is Horne who has set forth in more detail the evidence that establishes that Lifton was right.

When Air Force One landed at Andrews Air Force Base from Dallas, Kennedy's casket was placed into a gray Navy ambulance in which Kennedy's wife, Jacqueline, was traveling. Proceeding in a motorcade, the ambulance arrived at the front of the Bethesda Naval Hospital at 6:55 p.m.

At 8:00 p.m., a little more than an hour later, the casket was carried into the Bethesda morgue by a military honor team called the Joint Casket Bearer Team, which consisted of personnel from all the branches of military service, all of whom were in dress uniform and wore white gloves.

However, the evidence also establishes that at 6:35 p.m. — 90 minutes earlier than when Kennedy's Dallas casket was carried into the morgue at 8:00 p.m. by the Joint Casket Bearer Team — another group of military personnel carried the president's body into the Bethesda morgue. That casket was a plain shipping casket rather than the expensive, heavy, ornamental, bronze casket into which the president's body had been placed in Dallas.

Equally strange was the fact that the president's body at the 6:35 p.m. delivery was in a body bag rather than wrapped in the white sheets in which the medical personnel in Dallas had wrapped it before it was placed into the heavy, bronze casket in Dallas.

Have doubts? Let's look at the evidence.

On November 22, 1963, Marine Sgt. Roger Boyajian was stationed at the Marine Corps Institute in Washington, D.C. On that day, he received orders to go to the Bethesda Hospital to serve as NCO in charge of a 10-man Marine security detail for President Kennedy's autopsy.

Four days later — on November 26 — Boyajian filed a report of what happened. Here is what his report stated in part:

> The detail arrived at the hospital at approximately 1800 [6:00 p.m.] and after reporting as ordered several members of the detail were posted at entrances to prevent unauthorized persons from entering the prescribed area.... At approximately 1835 [6:35 p.m.] the casket was received at the morgue entrance and taken inside. (Bracketed material added.)

A copy of Sergeant Boyajian's report is available on the Internet as part of the online appendix to Horne's book (see https:www.fff.org/autopsy-references).

Still not convinced?

In 1963, E-6 Navy hospital corpsman Dennis David was stationed at the Bethesda National Navy Center, where his job consisted of reading medical textbooks and transforming them into Navy correspondence courses. David later became a Navy officer and served in that capacity for 11 years in the Medical Services Corps. He retired from active duty in 1976.

On November 22, 1963, David was serving as "Chief of the Day" at the Navy medical school at Bethesda. According to an official ARRB interview conducted by Horne on February 14, 1997, David stated that at about 5:30 p.m. he was summoned to appear at the office of the Chief of the Day for the entire Bethesda complex (including the medical school). When he arrived, there were three or four Secret Service agents in the office. He was informed that President Kennedy's autopsy was going to be held at the Bethesda morgue. David was ordered to round up a team, proceed to the morgue, and establish security. He rounded up several men from various barracks, proceeded to the Bethesda morgue, and assigned security duties to his team.

At around 6:30 p.m., David received a phone call stating that "your visitor is on the way: you will need some people to offload." David rounded up 7 or 8 sailors to carry in the casket and a few minutes later, a black hearse drove up. Several men in blue suits got out of the hearse, along with the driver and passenger, both of whom were wearing white (operating room) smocks. Under David's supervision, the sailors offloaded the casket and carried it into the morgue.

What did the casket look like? David stated that it was a simple, gray shipping casket similar to the ones commonly used in the Vietnam War.

Now keep in mind that the motorcade in which the gray Navy ambulance that carried Mrs. Kennedy and the heavy bronze casket into which her husband's body had been placed in Dallas didn't arrive at the hospital until 6:55 p.m., twenty minutes after Kennedy's body was carried into the morgue by David's team. Keep in mind also that according to the official version of events, the Dallas casket wasn't carried into the morgue by the Joint Casket Bearer Team until 8:00 p.m.

David added that after his team had delivered the shipping casket to the morgue, he proceeded into the main portion of the hospital, where several minutes later (i.e., at 6:55 p.m.) he saw the motorcade in which Mrs. Kennedy was traveling (and the Dallas casket was being transported) approaching the front of Bethesda Hospital. As he stated to Horne, he knew at that point that President Kennedy's body could not be in the Dallas casket because his team had, just a few minutes earlier, delivered Kennedy's body into the morgue in the shipping casket.

While David didn't personally witness the president's body being taken out of the shipping casket, he later asked one of the autopsy physicians, a U.S. Navy commander named Dr. J. Thornton Boswell, in which casket the president had come in. Boswell responded, "You ought to know; you were there."

Moreover, when Lifton showed David a photo of the Dallas casket in 1980, David categorically stated that that was not the shipping casket in which Kennedy's body had been delivered at 6:35 p.m. (Horne, volume 4, page 989).

What David told Horne in 1997 was a repetition of what David had told Lifton many years before, which Lifton had related in his 1981 book, *Best Evidence*. As Lifton recounts in his book, David gave the same account to a reporter from the Lake County *News-Sun* in Waukegan, Illinois, in 1975.

Horne's official ARRB report of his interview with David is available on the Internet at https://fff.org/autopsy-references. (Lifton's account is in Chapter 25 of his book and is entitled "The Lake County Informant.")

Still not satisfied?

According to Horne, "After *Best Evidence* was published, a Michigan newspaper and a Canadian news team located and interviewed Donald Rebentisch, one of the sailors in Dennis David's working party, who had been telling the same story independently for years" (Horne, volume 3, page 675).

So, you have a Marine sergeant and two sailors, whose statements unequivocally confirm that Kennedy's body was carried into the Bethesda morgue in a plain shipping casket at 6:35 p.m.

Is there any more evidence of the 6:35 p.m. delivery of Kennedy's body to the morgue?

Yes.

On November 22, 1963, Joseph Gawler's Sons, Inc., which, according to Horne, had been the most prestigious funeral home in Washington for many years, was summoned to Bethesda Hospital to perform the embalming of President Kennedy's body. On November 22–23, 1963, Gawler's prepared what was called a "First Call Sheet" for President Kennedy's autopsy, which contained the following handwritten notation:

"Body removed from metal shipping casket at NSNH at Bethesda."

The person who wrote that notation was Joseph E. Hagan, the supervisor in charge of the Gawler's embalming team for the Kennedy autopsy and who later became president of Gawler's. When the ARRB interviewed Hagan in 1996, he stated that he had not personally witnessed the president's body being brought into the morgue in the shipping casket but that someone whom he could not recall had advised him of that fact.

Gawler's First Call Sheet is available on the Internet at https://fff.org/autopsy-references.

Need more evidence?

Paul O'Connor was an E-4 Navy corpsman who served as an autopsy technician for the Kennedy autopsy on November 22, 1963. According to Horne, O'Connor told the House Select Committee on Assassinations in 1977 and Lifton in 1979 and 1980 that Kennedy's body had arrived in a "cheap, metal, aluminum" casket in a "rubberized body bag" with a "zipper down the middle" (Horne, volume 4, page 990).

In 1979, Lifton interviewed a man named Floyd Riebe, who was a medical photography student present at Kennedy's autopsy when he was an E-5 Navy corpsman stationed at Bethesda. According to Horne, Riebe stated that Kennedy's casket was not a viewing casket because the lid did not open halfway down. Riebe also confirmed that Kennedy's body was in a rubberized body bag with a zipper (Horne, volume 4, page 990).

Jerrol Custer was an E-4 Navy corpsman who served as an X-ray technician for the Kennedy autopsy. According to Horne, Custer told Lifton in repeated interviews that Kennedy's body was in a body bag. Custer also told Lifton that he saw the black hearse that brought in the shipping casket. He stated that he saw two different caskets in the Bethesda morgue, one of which was bronze. Interestingly, in a deposition conducted by the ARRB in 1997, Custer denied that Kennedy was in a body bag even though he had stated the contrary in two separate interviews with Lifton in 1979 and 1989 (Horne, volume 4, page 991).

Ed Reed, an E-4 Navy corpsman, also served as an X-ray technician for the Kennedy autopsy. In an ARRB deposition in 1997, Reed testified that Kennedy's casket was a "typical aluminum military casket." He said that there were Marines present at the time the casket was delivered. He recalled that the president arrived in a see-through clear plastic bag, not in a standard body bag (Horne, volume 4, page 991).

According to Horne, James Jenkins, another E-4 Navy corpsman who served as an autopsy technician for Kennedy's autopsy, told Lifton in 1979 that Kennedy's casket was not ornamental and that it was plain — "awful clean and simple" and "not something you'd expect a president to be in" (Horne, volume 4, page 992).

According to Horne, John VanHuesen, a member of the Gawler's embalming team, told the ARRB that he recalled seeing a "black, zippered plastic pouch" in the Bethesda morgue early in the autopsy (Horne, volume 4, page 992).

So, what do we have here? We have eight Marine and Navy enlisted personnel who were performing their assigned duties on November 22, 1963, and whose statements unequivocally establish that Kennedy's body was delivered to the Bethesda morgue at 6:35 p.m. in a shipping casket and in a body bag rather than in the heavy, ornamental, bronze casket into which it had been placed at Parkland Hospital, wrapped in white sheets.

We also have two written reports — Sergeant Boyajian's report and the Gawler's report — that were filed contemporaneously with the autopsy, both of which confirm the early arrival of Kennedy's body in the shipping casket. We also have a member of the Gawler's embalming team stating that he saw a body bag in the morgue.

But that's not all. We also have the statement by Dennis David that after he and his team offloaded Kennedy's casket and delivered it into the morgue at 6:35 p.m., he personally witnessed the motorcade in which Mrs. Kennedy (and the Dallas casket) was traveling approaching the front of Bethesda Hospital at 6:55 p.m.

In fact, David isn't the only one who saw Mrs. Kennedy's motorcade (which contained the Dallas casket) approaching Bethesda Hospital after the president's body had already been delivered to the morgue at 6:35 p.m. According to Horne, Jerrol Custer told Lifton in 1980 that he had seen Mrs. Kennedy in the main lobby while he was on his way upstairs to process X-rays that had already been taken of the president's body (Horne, volume 4, page 991).

Let's now turn back to the official version of events. The official version is that Kennedy's body was carried into the Bethesda morgue by the Joint Casket Bearer Team at 8:00 p.m. in the heavy, ornamental, bronze casket into which it had been placed at Parkland Hospital. This is the account given in William Manchester's book *The Death of a President*. When the casket was opened, Kennedy's body was taken out, and witnesses confirmed that it was wrapped in the white sheets that had been wrapped around the body by the Parkland Hospital personnel in Dallas. At 8:15 p.m., the autopsy began.

So, which is it?

Was Kennedy's body carried by a team of sailors into the Bethesda morgue at 6:35 p.m. in a shipping casket encased in a body bag after being delivered in a black hearse that contained several men in blue suits?

Or was it carried in by the Joint Casket Bearer Team at 8:00 p.m. in the heavy, ornamental, bronze casket from Dallas and wrapped in white sheets after being delivered in a gray Navy ambulance?

The answer: Both.

Now, I know what you're thinking: "There's no way that Kennedy's body would have been delivered two different times into the Bethesda morgue. Why would anyone do that? Anyway, if Kennedy's body was actually delivered into the morgue at 6:35 p.m. in the shipping casket, how did it get back into the heavy, ornamental, bronze casket from Dallas that the Joint Casket Bearer Team carried in at 8:00 p.m.? Why, that's just plain crazy!"

Permit me to cite some of the adjectives that the noted attorney Vincent Bugliosi used in a chapter entitled "David Lifton and the Alteration of the President's Body" in his book *Reclaiming History: The Assassination of President John F. Kennedy*: "preposterous," "far out," "unhinged," and "nonsense."

So, which casket delivery would you guess Bugliosi settled on — the 6:35 p.m. delivery of the shipping casket with the body bag or the 8:00 p.m. heavy bronze casket delivery with the white sheets wrapped around Kennedy's body?

You guessed wrong!

Bugliosi settled on a third casket delivery.

Yes, you read that right. Vincent Bugliosi, along with noted conspiracy critic Gerald Posner, author of the 1993 book *Case Closed: Lee Harvey Oswald and the Assassination of JFK*, have settled on a third casket delivery into the Bethesda morgue — one that took place between 7:00 p.m. and 7:30 p.m. — that is, after the 6:35 p.m. casket delivery and before the 8:00 p.m. casket delivery.

Are you doubting me? Are you thinking to yourself, "No way, Jacob! Two casket deliveries were already enough for me. But a third? Now you've gone too far!"?

Permit me first to set forth Bugliosi's position. Referring to Paul O'Connor, the E-4 X-ray technician cited above, Bugliosi writes:

O'Connor told the HSCA [House Select Committee on Assassinations] investigators that the president's body arrived in a pink shipping casket and told Lifton that the body arrived in a "cheap, pinkish gray casket, just a tin box." But FBI agent James Sibert told me that he, his partner, Francis O'Neill, a few Secret Service agents, and a few others he doesn't recall, carried the casket from the limousine at the back of the hospital to "an anteroom right next to the autopsy room...." He vividly remembers that "it was a very expensive one, definitely not a shipping casket" and he recalls it was "very, very heavy...." [The] November 26, 1963, report of FBI agents Sibert and O'Neill reads that when the president's body arrived in the autopsy room, "the complete body was wrapped in sheets".... (Bugliosi, pages 1069–70; bracketed material added).

Posner writes:

Sibert and O'Neill helped take the casket inside, and there, waiting for the President's body were [autopsy physicians] Dr. James Humes and Dr. J. Thornton Boswell.... When the funeral motorcade arrived at the hospital, Robert and Jacqueline Kennedy were escorted to upstairs waiting rooms while the casket was brought to the morgue. There, Drs. Humes and Boswell, with help from FBI agents O'Neill and Sibert and Secret Service agents Kellerman and Greer, removed the body.... (Posner, chapter 13, page 299; bracketed material added).

Having concluded that the president's casket could have been delivered only one time to the Bethesda morgue, Bugliosi and Posner obviously concluded that FBI agents Francis O'Neill and James Sibert and Secret Service agents Roy Kellerman and William Greer must be the only ones telling the truth and that the enlisted men who stated they carried the president's body into the morgue at 6:35 p.m. in a shipping casket had to be speaking falsely.

It is clear that to both Bugliosi and Posner it is inconceivable that the 6:35 p.m. group could be telling the truth. Bugliosi ridicules the veracity of Paul O'Connor, while Posner mocks the veracity of O'Connor, Jerrol Custer, and James Jenkins.

What about Marine Sgt. Roger Boyajian, who filed the after-action report on November 26, in which he stated unequivocally that the president's casket had been carried into the morgue at 6:35 p.m.?

What about Dennis David, the Chief of Day for the Naval medical school, who later retired from the Navy as an officer, who stated that the president's body had been carried into the morgue at 6:35 p.m. in a shipping casket?

What about Donald Rebentisch, a member of David's team, who stated the same thing?

What about Floyd Riebe and Ed Reed, two other enlisted men who confirmed the account?

What about Joseph Gawler's Sons, Inc., whose representatives filed a written report on November 22–23, 1963, which stated that the president's body had arrived in a shipping casket?

Most of them aren't even mentioned by Bugliosi and Posner, and Posner describes them collectively as "bit players at Bethesda — orderlies, technicians, and casket carriers."

Bit players?

Permit me to level a very simple question at Vincent Bugliosi and Gerald Posner: Why in the world would these eight enlisted men, who were simply doing their jobs on the evening of November 22, 1963, have any reason to lie or concoct a false story about bringing the president's body into the Bethesda morgue?

Only Bugliosi and Posner can explain why they didn't carefully focus on and analyze the statements and testimony of all these witnesses but let me give you my theory on the matter. In my opinion, the reason they didn't do so is that they knew that if they did, their position would immediately become untenable.

Why?

Because both Bugliosi and Posner know that the chance that each of all those witnesses came up with the same fake story independently of all the other witnesses who were saying the same thing is so astronomically small as to be nonexistent.

Therefore, for all the witnesses to have all come up with the same fake story about the 6:35 p.m. delivery of Kennedy's body into the Bethesda morgue in a shipping casket would have had to involve one of the most preposterous conspiracies of all time. Bugliosi and Posner would be relegated to becoming conspiracy theorists and ridiculous ones at that. They would be alleging that eight enlisted men in the United States Armed Forces who were suddenly called to duty to serve at the autopsy of President John F. Kennedy's body conspired to concoct a wild and fake story about how they delivered President Kennedy's body into the Bethesda morgue in a shipping casket at 6:35 p.m. on the evening of November 22, 1963. Oh, I forgot — the conspiracy also would have included the most prestigious funeral home in Washington, D.C., the funeral home that the U.S. military had selected to handle the embalming of the president's body.

Well, pray tell, Messrs.. Bugliosi and Posner: What would have been the motive behind such a conspiracy?

Perhaps if we try to imagine how the conspiracy got arranged, we can figure out what the motive was.

Let's see: Carrying out his orders to establish a team of Marines for security at Bethesda Hospital, Marine Sgt. Boyajian calls the team together and says, "Men, I've got an idea. Let's conspire to come up with a fake and false story about how the president's body got delivered to the Bethesda morgue. We'll tell everybody that his body was brought to the morgue in a black hearse that contained several men in blue suits and that Kennedy's body was contained in a shipping casket and a body bag." The team goes along with the idea.

Then, once Marine Sergeant Boyajian arrives at the morgue, he collars the Chief of the Day at Bethesda Medical School, Dennis David (a "bit player" who would later become a Navy officer), and whispers in his ear, "Hey, dude, my Marines and I have come up with a great idea. We're conspiring to concoct a fake story about how we delivered President Kennedy's body into the morgue in a shipping casket at 6:35 p.m. Would you like to join our conspiracy?"

David responds, "Wow! That sounds great! Yeah, I'll talk to my team about it." So David goes to his team and convinces them to join the conspiracy.

Oh, but wait — there are also the other "bit players" to contact. So, the conspirators approach the X-ray technicians and photographers and, after some persuasion, convince them to join the conspiracy.

All that's left is Joseph Gawler's Sons, Inc. No problem. When they hear about the idea, they think it's fantastic, and they're willing to risk the good reputation they've built up over the years to become the most prestigious funeral home in Washington and quickly join the conspiracy.

And for what? Whoops! It still isn't clear what the motive of all those "orderlies, technicians, and casket carriers" could have been.

Let me use the adjectives that Bugliosi employed to describe this supposed conspiracy among what Posner described as "bit players": "preposterous," "far out," "unhinged," and "nonsense."

Unless one is convinced that such an impossible conspiracy took place, there is only one conclusion that can be reached: Those eight enlisted men and the representatives of Gawler's funeral home, all of whom were suddenly and unexpectedly called to do their duty on the evening of November 22, 1963, were telling the truth. President Kennedy's body was carried into the Bethesda morgue at 6:35 p.m. in a shipping casket and inside a body bag.

The next question naturally arises: Was the O'Neill-Sibert-Kellerman-Greer casket delivery that Bugliosi and Posner settled on the same casket delivery as the Joint Casket Bearer's Team's casket delivery? Or were they two separate casket deliveries?

Posner doesn't address the issue. In fact, he doesn't even mention the Joint Casket Bearer's Team's delivery of the Dallas casket, which would seem odd, since it was prominently mentioned in William Manchester's famous book on the assassination, *The Death of a President*. Perhaps Posner had difficulty reconciling the two different accounts and just felt it would be simpler to leave one of them out of his analysis.

Bugliosi, on the other hand, does address the issue. What is his approach? Obviously convinced that there could have been only one casket delivery that night, he conflates the O'Neill-Sibert-Kellerman-Greer casket delivery and the Joint Casket Bearer Team's casket delivery into one casket delivery.

The problem for Bugliosi, however, is that the evidence does not support his position. Instead, the evidence leads to but one conclusion: three separate casket deliveries, as follows:

6:35 p.m. — First casket delivery. We know this from the statements of Marine Sergeant Boyajian, Chief of the Day David, the six other enlisted men, and the Gawler's funeral home report.

Between 7:00 p.m. and 7:30 p.m. — Second casket delivery. We know this from statements made by FBI agents O'Neill and Sibert and Secret Service agent Kellerman, as shown below.

8:00 p.m. — Third casket delivery. We know this from the official report of the Joint Casket Bearer's Team, as shown below.

We have already reviewed the evidence that establishes the first casket delivery and its time of delivery of 6:35 p.m.

Let's now review the evidence that establishes the second casket delivery, which took place sometime between 7:00 p.m. and 7:30 p.m.

In their official report of November 26, 1963, O'Neill and Sibert stated in part as follows:

> On arrival at the Medical Center, the ambulance stopped in front of the main entrance, at which time Mrs. Jacqueline Kennedy and Attorney General Robert Kennedy embarked from the ambulance and entered the building. The ambulance was thereafter driven around to the rear entrance where the President's body was removed and taken into an

autopsy room. Bureau agents assisted in the moving of the casket to the autopsy room.

Keep in mind that the ambulance arrived in the front of the hospital at 6:55 p.m. Keep in mind also that the Joint Casket Bearer Team didn't deliver the Dallas casket to the morgue until more than an hour later, at 8:00 p.m.

On March 12, 1964, an official memo of the Warren Commission recounted the following exchange between Warren Commission counsel Arlen Spector and FBI agents O'Neill and Sibert:

Question: What was the time of the preparation for the autopsy at the hospital?
Answer: Approximately 7:17 p.m.
Question: What time did the autopsy begin?
Answer: Approximately 8:15 p.m.

Ask yourself: How could preparation for the autopsy begin at approximately 7:17 p.m. if the Joint Casket Bearer Team didn't deliver the body into the morgue until 8:00 p.m.? Of course, since we know that the body had already been delivered to the morgue at 6:35 p.m. in the shipping casket, preparation for the autopsy could have begun at 7:17 p.m.

In fact, recall that X-ray technician Jerrol Custer, one of the enlisted men who witnessed Kennedy's body being brought into the morgue in the shipping casket, saw Mrs. Kennedy entering the main lobby of the hospital as Custer was heading upstairs to process X-rays of Kennedy's body.

Question: How could Custer have been processing X-rays of the president's body if the Dallas casket containing the president's body had not yet been delivered by either the Joint Casket Delivery Team at 8:00 p.m. or by O'Neill, Sibert, Kellerman, and Greer sometime between 7:00 p.m. and 7:30 p.m.?

In a deposition that was taken by the ARRB in 1997, Sibert was asked about the 7:17 p.m. time that he and O'Neill had referred to in their 1964 exchange with Specter:

Gunn: I will read for the record, if you will read along with me. "Question: What was the time of the preparation for the autopsy at the hospital?" "Answer: Approximately 7:17 P.M." Do you see those words?
Sibert: Yes.

[...]

Gunn: Well, I guess my question in part is: Does the time that is provided here, 7:17 P.M., help you identify the approximate time that the casket was unloaded from the Navy ambulance?

Sibert: Well, that could have been the time that it was unloaded, the 7:17 — or just a short time thereafter when they got it in there. And, of course, they had to take the body out of the casket, put it on the autopsy table and this would be all the preparation too. (Horne, volume 3, pages 713–14).

Ask yourself: If there was only one casket delivery, how could it be unloaded at 7:17 p.m. and also 8:00 p.m., as reported by the Joint Casket Bearer Team?

Here is what O'Neill wrote in a sworn statement to the House Select Committee on Assassinations in 1978:

Upon arriving at the National Naval Medical Center of Bethesda, the ambulance stopped at the front entrance where Jackie and RFK disembarked to proceed to the 17th floor. The ambulance then travelled to the rear where Sibert, Bill Greer (Secret Service), and Roy Kellerman (Secret Service), and I placed the casket on a roller and transported it into the autopsy room.

Notice that, once again, the implication is that the casket is promptly delivered after the 6:55 p.m. arrival of the motorcade. Also, notice that there is no mention of the Joint Casket Bearer Team and that O'Neill states that he, Sibert, Greer, and Kellerman transported the casket into the morgue *on a roller.*

In an affidavit signed and delivered to the House Select Committee on Assassinations in 1978, Sibert reinforced O'Neill's testimony:

When the motorcade from the airport arrived at the Naval Hospital, Bobby Kennedy and Mrs. Kennedy were let off at the administration building. Mr. O'Neill and I helped carry the damaged casket into the autopsy room with some Secret Service agents.

Consider the testimony of Secret Service Agent Kellerman before the Warren Commission in 1964:

Mr. Specter: What time did that autopsy start, as you recollect it?

Mr. Kellerman: Immediately. Immediately after we brought him in.

Later in his testimony, Kellerman became more specific:

Mr. Kellerman: Let's come back to the period of our arrival at Andrews Air Force Base, which was 5:58 p.m. at night. By the time it took us to take the body from the plane into the ambulance, and a couple of carloads of staff people who followed us, we may have spent 15 minutes there. And in driving from Andrews to the U.S. Naval Hospital, I would judge, a good 45 minutes. So, there is 7 o'clock. We went immediately over, without too much delay on the outside of the hospital, into the morgue. The Navy people had their staff in readiness right then. There wasn't anybody to call. They were all there. So, at the latest, 7:30, they began to work on the autopsy....

Notice that Kellerman is reinforcing O'Neill's and Sibert's testimony that they delivered the Dallas casket into the morgue sometime between 7:00 p.m. and 7:30 p.m. Ask yourself: How could they begin to work on the autopsy no later than 7:30 p.m., given that the Joint Casket Bearer Team didn't deliver the Dallas casket until 8:00 p.m.?

According to Horne, a *Washington Star* article dated November 23, 1963, referring to the motorcade's 6:55 p.m. (or 6:53 p.m., as another account asserted) arrival at the front of the Bethesda Hospital with Mrs. Kennedy and the Dallas casket, "also noted that the ambulance containing the casket was not driven away from the front of the hospital facility for at least 12 minutes after it arrived, i.e., at about 7:07 p.m. (or at 7:05 p.m. at the earliest, depending on which arrival time one uses)" (Horne, volume 3, pages 677–78). That fits with O'Neill's, Sibert's, and Kellerman's testimony that the Dallas casket was delivered to the morgue between 7:00 p.m. and 7:30 p.m.

Let's now review the evidence that establishes the third casket delivery, the one at 8:00 p.m. by the Joint Casket Bearer Team.

Headed by infantry 1st Lt. Samuel Bird, the Joint Casket Bearer Team was the honor team charged with formally carrying President Kennedy's body into the Bethesda morgue. As previously stated, the team consisted of soldiers in dress uniform and white gloves representing all the branches of the military.

On December 10, 1963, Lt. Bird filed his official report of the Joint Casket Bearer Team's delivery of the president's casket into the Bethesda morgue on the evening of November 22, 1963. The report stated in part:

> The Joint Casket Team consisted of one officer, one NCO and seven enlisted men (from each branch of the Armed Forces).... They removed the remains as follows: 1. From the ambulance to the morgue (Bethesda) 2000 hours [8:00 p.m.], 22 Nov. 63. (Bracketed material added.)

A copy of the Joint Casket Bearer Team's official report is available on the Internet (see https://fff.org/autopsy-references).

You will notice that the report makes no mention of O'Neill, Sibert, Kellerman, or Greer or the roller that O'Neill, Sibert, Kellerman, and Greer used to carry the casket into the morgue.

You'll also notice that the report contains the following memorable incident, later recounted in Manchester's *The Death of a President:*

> While the casket was being moved inside the hospital, Brigadier General [Godfrey] McHugh relieved [illegible] from the casket team and awkwardly took his place. (Bracketed material added).

Nowhere do O'Neill, Sibert, Kellerman, or Greer relate the McHugh incident in their account of delivering the Dallas casket into the morgue.

There is something else to consider: A member of the Joint Casket Bearer Team denied that O'Neill, Sibert, Kellerman, and Greer helped the team carry the casket into the morgue. According to Lifton,

> I asked Cheek [a member of the Joint Casket Bearer Team] whether two FBI men were present when the ambulance was unloaded. "No," he replied, "there were just the six of us." I asked this because Sibert and O'Neill reported they helped with the casket, but made no mention of a casket team (Lifton, chapter 16; bracketed material added).

Now, consider the following sworn testimony before the Warren Commission on March 16, 1964, of Commander James J. Humes, one of the physicians who conducted the autopsy on the president's body on the evening of November 22:

Mr. Specter: What time did the autopsy start approximately?

> **Commander Humes:** The president's body was received at 25 minutes
> before 8, and the autopsy began at approximately 8 p.m. on that
> evening (Warren Commission Report, volume 2, page 349).

Ask yourself: How could the body have been received at 7:35 p.m. (i.e., 25 minutes before 8:00 p.m.) if the Joint Casket Bearer's Team didn't deliver it until 8:00 p.m.?

Now, let's examine the thesis originally developed by Lifton and later expanded upon by Horne to see if the evidence is consistent with three casket deliveries into the morgue.

Again, unless one concludes that Marine Sergeant Boyajian, Chief of the Day David, the other six enlisted men, and Gawler's funeral home entered into a quick, preposterous conspiracy to concoct a fake story about the delivery of the president's body, we begin with the fact that President Kennedy's body was offloaded from a black hearse containing several men in blue suits and delivered into the Bethesda morgue in a shipping casket at 6:35 p.m.

That obviously means that the Dallas casket that arrived twenty minutes later at 6:55 p.m. in the motorcade with Mrs. Kennedy did not contain the president's body.

Therefore, there was an obvious challenge for whoever did this and wished to keep it secret: how to get the president's body back into the Dallas casket so that it could be formally delivered into the morgue by the Joint Casket Bearer Team just before the autopsy would begin?

As Horne explains, that was what the O'Neill-Sibert-Kellerman-Greer casket delivery had to be all about. Soon after the arrival of the motorcade, they drove around to the morgue and carried the empty Dallas casket into the morgue sometime between 7:00 p.m. and 7:30 p.m.

Then, sometime between 7:30 p.m. and 8:00 p.m., the president's body was then wrapped back into the white sheets in which it had been wrapped in Dallas, placed back into the Dallas casket, and carried back out to the Navy ambulance, enabling the Joint Casket Bearer Team to officially carry it back into the morgue at 8:00 p.m.

There is actually no other reasonable conclusion that can be drawn from the evidence. Kennedy's body is delivered at 6:35 p.m. in the shipping casket. The middle delivery of the Dallas casket — the one between 7:00 p.m. and 7:30 p.m. — was used to effect the transfer of the body back into the Dallas casket, so that it can then be carried back out into the gray ambulance and then be delivered formally into the morgue at 8:00 p.m. by the Joint Casket Bearer Team, enabling the autopsy to formally begin 8:15 p.m., which is the time that everyone agrees the autopsy formally began.

Why was all this done? That is a very good question.

One possible explanation is that officials were concerned about the possibility that someone might try to attack the motorcade from Andrews Air Force Base to Bethesda Hospital and steal the president's body and, therefore, decided to secretly separate the president's body from the Dallas casket and secretly transport it to the morgue to obviate that possibility.

It seems to me that that would have been a plausible explanation if they had announced it publicly at the time. But they didn't do that. Instead, they engaged in secrecy, deception, and cover-up, and have ever since.

Some people would undoubtedly respond, "No way, Jacob! Not high government officials. They would never lie to the American people. Only 'bit players' like Marine sergeants, Navy enlisted men, and long-established funeral homes would do that."

But keep in mind that it is undisputed that several months after the events at Bethesda Naval Hospital, it wasn't "bit players" consisting of "orderlies, technicians, and casket carriers" who secretly conspired to concoct a fake story about a North Vietnamese attack at the Gulf of Tonkin, with the intent of securing a congressional resolution that would lead to the Vietnam War. Instead, it was the new president of the United States, Lyndon B. Johnson, and the entire Joint Chiefs of Staff, who entered into that secret and deadly conspiracy.

It seems to me that if high government officials would conspire to lie about a military attack that they had to know would bring on a war that would result in the deaths of tens of thousands of American soldiers (and millions of Vietnamese people), high government officials would be fully capable of lying about casket deliveries on the night of November 22, 1963.

The only other explanation for the multiple casket delivery that I can conceive of is a nefarious one, the one that is carefully detailed by Horne: that U.S. military officials at the Bethesda morgue, including the autopsy physicians, perhaps following orders based on national security, used the period of time from 6:35 p.m. to 8:00 p.m. on the night of the autopsy to alter the president's body in order to hide any evidence of wounds resulting from gunshots that came from the front of the president, e.g., from the grassy knoll.

One of the most fascinating stories that Horne describes involves the testimony of Tom Robinson, a member of the Gawler's embalming team. When Robinson was questioned by the House Select Committee on Assassinations, he made the following cryptic statement:

> The time that the people moved (autopsy). The body was taken ... and the body never came ... lots of little things like that (Horne, volume 2, page 607).

Those are not my ellipses. They are also not Horne's. In fact, neither are the parentheses around the word "autopsy." That's exactly how Robinson's testimony appears in the official transcript of his testimony. As Horne points out, that's fairly unusual, given that people don't ordinarily speak using ellipses and parentheses. Those sorts of things are used in written communications, not oral ones.

Because Robinson's testimony was recorded, Horne decided to look up the tape and listen to the actual recording of Robinson's testimony. His office located the tape labeled as Robinson's testimony in the National Archives. Unfortunately, however, the tape contained something else on it, and Horne was not able to locate another tape with Robinson's testimony on it.

Perhaps I should mention that after Robinson gave his testimony, it was ordered sealed for 50 years, along with testimony provided by other people for the House Select Committee on Assassinations. Keep in mind also that the Warren Commission had ordered many of its records sealed for 75 years. It was only thanks to the JFK Records Act, enacted in the wake of Oliver Stone's movie *JFK*, that such records were ordered to be opened to the public.

The pertinent excerpt from the official transcript of Robinson's testimony is available on the Internet (see https://fff.org/autopsy-references).

It might interest you to know that the personnel who participated in Kennedy's autopsy, both military and civilian, were required by U.S. military officials to sign written oaths of secrecy in which they promised to never reveal what they had witnessed at the autopsy, on threat of court martial or criminal prosecution.

In fact, as Horne pointed out:

> A considerable amount of effort by the HSCA's Chief Counsel, Robert Blakey, was required to get the Pentagon to lift the gag order during the late 1970s. Even then, some participants at the autopsy (such as James

Curtis Jenkins) were hesitant to talk about what they had witnessed, and others (such as Jerrol Custer) still stubbornly refused. Many of the enlisted men present in the morgue, as well as civilian photographer John Stringer, have recalled quite vividly the threatening manner in which this letter was delivered to them by CAPT Stover, Humes' immediate superior and the Commanding Officer of the Naval Medical School at Bethesda (Horne, volume 1, page xxvii).

If you would like to see a copy of the oath of secrecy that people were required to sign, it is available on MaryFerrell.org (see https:www.fff.org/autopsy-references).

Do you now see why the authors of *The Kennedy Detail: JFK's Secret Service Agents Break Their Silence* might have chosen to omit a detailed account of what happened at Bethesda Hospital on the evening of November 22, 1963, notwithstanding their promise to "reveal the inside story of the assassination, the weeks and days that led to it and its heartrending aftermath"? Specifically denying Lifton's (and Horne's) contention that President Kennedy's body had been "kidnapped" (the term used by the authors) and omitting any reference whatsoever to Lt. Bird and his Joint Casket Bearer Team, the sum total of the authors' account of what happened at the Bethesda morgue that night was the following sentence: "There was a presidential suite on the seventeenth floor of the hospital, and as Bill Greer, Roy Kellerman, and Admiral Burkley accompanied the casket to the morgue for the autopsy, Clint Hill and Paul Landis escorted Mrs. Kennedy and her brother-in-law the attorney general to the suite" (Blaine and McCubbin, Chapters 15 and 22).

Regardless of whether one believes that President Kennedy was killed by a lone-nut assassin or was the victim of a conspiracy, the American people have a right to know exactly what happened at Bethesda Hospital on November 22, 1963, and why.

Who were the men in blue suits who got out of the black hearse that delivered the president's body in a shipping casket at 6:35 p.m.? What were their names and who did they work for? Were they Secret Service, FBI, or CIA? Are they still alive and, if so, where are they? Did they file written reports of their actions on that evening and, if so, where are those reports today? Why, when, and how was Kennedy's body separated from the Dallas casket? Why all the secrecy and deception associated with the delivery of the president's body into the Bethesda morgue?

Although President John F. Kennedy's autopsy took place almost 50 years ago, we the people — the citizens of the United States living today — have a right to know everything about what happened on the night of November 22, 1963, and why. Notwithstanding the lapse of almost half a century, U.S. government officials, including those in the Pentagon, the Secret Service, the FBI, and the CIA, have a duty to provide us with the complete truth.

B

The Shot That Killed Kennedy

In October 2010 I wrote an article entitled "The Kennedy Casket Conspiracy" in which I detailed the strange circumstances surrounding the delivery of President John F. Kennedy's body to the morgue at Bethesda Naval Hospital after the fatal shooting in Dallas in November 1963. This article is included as Appendix B of this book. My article was based mostly on the evidence presented in Douglas P. Horne's 2009 five-volume work on the assassination, *Inside the Assassination Records Review Board: The U.S. Government's Final Attempt to Reconcile the Conflicting Medical Evidence in the Assassination of JFK*, which in turn was based on the 1981 bestselling book on the assassination, *Best Evidence*, by David Lifton.

My article detailed the evidence establishing that there were actually three different casket deliveries to the Bethesda morgue on the evening of November 22, 1963, with the earliest casket delivery — the one that high U.S. officials have long denied took place — occurring at 6:35 p.m., almost 1 hour and 45 minutes before the autopsy officially began at 8:15 p.m.

The evidence, as documented in Lifton's and Horne's books, consisted of the statements of several enlisted military men who were charged with security at the morgue and with carrying the body into the morgue, as well as contemporaneous official reports that had been kept secret for decades, until they were released in the 1990s pursuant to the new law, the JFK Records Act, that was enacted in the wake of Oliver Stone's 1991 movie, *JFK*.

As I stated in my article, the possibility that all the enlisted men and all the people who prepared the official reports entered into a conspiracy on the day of the assassination to concoct a fake and false story about the time and circumstances that the president's body was delivered to the morgue is so preposterous as to be nonexistent.

Since my article was published, not a single person has written me alleging that I got any of the facts in the matter wrong or that the conclusions I drew from the facts were incorrect. A couple of people did call me a conspiracy theorist. Duh! The title of my article was "The Kennedy

Casket Conspiracy." Since the early, secret delivery of Kennedy's body to the Bethesda morgue involved several people, the matter necessarily involved a conspiracy — by definition.

If you haven't read my article "The Kennedy Casket Conspiracy," I invite you to do so. It's long, but necessarily so because it pulls together the overwhelming weight of evidence showing that government officials secretly and surreptitiously delivered President Kennedy's body to the Bethesda morgue an hour and a half before the autopsy officially began.

Now, you might say, "Jacob, all that is fine and good. But was there anything unusual about the autopsy itself that would make this information important?"

Well, as a matter of fact, yes. In fact, there are many unusual aspects to the president's autopsy, which was entirely controlled by the U.S. military.

Let's consider, for example, the headshot, the fatal wound that brought an end to the president's life.

Immediately after the assassination, the doctors and nurses at Parkland Hospital in Dallas, where the president was treated, made note of a hole in the back of Kennedy's head that was approximately 2 or 3 inches in diameter. The hole was primarily in the lower part of the back of the head.

Is the size of such a hole significant? Yes, owing to the manner in which a bullet enters and exits a solid mass. When a bullet enters, say, a person's head, it creates a very small hole, like the size of the bullet itself. But as it passes through the brain, it pushes mass in front of it and also begins to tumble. Thus, by the time it exits, it leaves a hole much larger than the entry hole.

Let's review what the Dallas physicians stated about Kennedy's head wound. According to Lifton (page 317):

Indeed, six Dallas doctors testified the wound in the head was an exit wound; and a seventh, Dr. Kemp Clark, said it *could* be an exit wound but it was also possible the wound was "tangential"; Dr. Jones testified it "appeared to be an exit wound in the posterior portion of the skull"; Dr. Perry referred to it as "avulsive"; Dr. Jenkins, referring to the region as "exploded," said, "I would interpret it as being a wound of exit"; and Dr. Akin said, "I assume that the right occipitoparietal [lower right rear of head] region was the exit." [Text in brackets added.]

Lifton relates Dr. Robert McClelland's testimony before the Warren Commission:

> As I took the position at the head of the table ... I was in such a position that I could very closely examine the head wound, and I noted that the right posterior portion of the skull had been extremely blasted. It has been shattered, apparently, by the force of the shot.... This sprung open the bones ... in such a way that you could actually look down into the skull cavity itself and see that probably a third or so, at least, of the brain tissue, posterior cerebral tissue and some of the cerebellar tissue had been blasted out. So, what's the problem? Well, take a look at a copy of one of the official autopsy photographs of the back of Kennedy's head. As you can see, you are not looking at anything gruesome.

Do you see the problem? At the risk of belaboring the obvious, what purports to be an official autopsy photograph of the back of President Kennedy's head clearly does not show the big exit hole that the Dallas doctors stated was there in the back of the head. In fact, according to the official version of events, that official autopsy photograph depicts a small entry wound, which then exited in a large blow-out wound in the top of Kennedy's head.

The difference between what the Parkland doctors saw and what the autopsy photograph shows is obviously of critical importance.

If the Parkland doctors are correct, then there are two inevitable conclusions:

One, the government's official photographs of the president's body had to have been faked, and two, accused assassin Lee Harvey Oswald could not have been the one who shot President Kennedy in the head, given that he was supposed to have fired from behind the president while the president was facing forward.

If, on the other hand, the photographs correctly depict the back of the president's head, then there are two inevitable conclusions: the Dallas doctors either entered into a conspiracy to falsify the location of the wound or they simply imagined a wound that didn't actually exist.

But the possibility that the doctors knowingly conspired with each other to concoct a fake and false wound is as preposterous as the possibility that the enlisted men and morticians in Bethesda conspired to concoct a fake and false story of when the president's body was delivered to the Bethesda morgue.

But before you jump to the conclusion that the Dallas doctors must have imagined a big exit wound at the back of Kennedy's head that didn't really exist, keep in mind that Parkland Hospital was — and still is — one of the most renowned trauma centers in the United States. In fact, it is among the largest teaching hospitals in the country. If a person gets shot, there is hardly a better, more competent place to be treated than Parkland Hospital.

What about the doctors at the Bethesda morgue, the ones who were at the autopsy that night? What did they say about the head wound?

In 1976 the House Select Committee on Assassinations (HSCA) conducted an official investigation into the assassination of President Kennedy, owing to widespread doubts among the public about the Warren Commission's official report in 1964. The final report of the House Committee stated in part as follows:

In disagreement with the observations of the Parkland doctors are the 26 people present at the autopsy. All of those interviewed who attended the autopsy corroborated the general location of the wounds as depicted in the photographs; none had differing accounts.

So, there you have it: the Parkland doctors versus the Bethesda doctors.

Well, except for one big thing. Whoever it was that drafted that particular paragraph was a liar.

The last thing the House Select Committee anticipated was that anyone would find that the Committee was lying when it made that statement because the Committee specifically ordered that the evidence in the case, including the evidence that would expose the lie, would remain secret for 50 years. Apparently, they were as concerned with "national security" as the Warren Commission, which had ordered its evidence about the assassination sealed for 75 years. Of course, everyone knows that by the time 50 years or 75 years pass, most, if not all, of the pertinent evidence would probably have disappeared or been destroyed.

Oliver Stone changed all those plans with his movie *JFK*. Thanks to the movie and the resulting JFK Records Act, the Assassination Records Review Board (ARRB), on which Douglas Horne served, was able to bring the House Select Committee records into the public eye.

And guess what? The records showed that that particular portion of the Committee's official report was one great big lie. Horne writes (volume 3, page 886):

One might well ask how I can be so sure that this statement was a falsehood, and not just a "mistake." Here is why — the autopsy photos show the back of the head to be intact, and yet the following autopsy witnesses interviewed by the HSCA indicated that it was *not*.... [Emphasis in original.]

Horne then proceeds to show a chart listing the following federal personnel who attended the Bethesda autopsy and the manner in which they disagreed with the autopsy photos and the source for their respective testimonies: HMC Chester H. Boyles; HM3 Jan G. Rudnicki; HM3 James E. Metzler; LCDR Gregory H. Cross, M.D.; HM3 Edward F. Reed; HM3 Paul K. O'Connor; HM3 James C. Jenkins; LCDR John H. Ebersole, M.D.; FBI Agent Frank O'Neill; FBI agent Jim Sibert; and U.S. Secret Service agent Roy Kellerman.

Anyone else?

Well, yes. Do you recall that Secret Service agent, Clint Hill, who crawled up on the back of the Kennedy limousine and pushed Jacqueline Kennedy back into the car? He got a good look at the back of the president's head while he was shielding the president and Mrs. Kennedy in the back seat while on the way to Parkland Hospital. Here is what he stated (Lifton, page 39), "The right rear portion of the head was missing. It was lying in the rear seat of the car. His brain was exposed."

According to Horne (volume 1, page xxxix), "In the HSCA transcript, [mortician] Tom Robinson describes a round defect in the rear of President Kennedy's head about the size of a small orange — three inches in diameter."

Anyone else?

Well, yes. According to Horne (volume 1, page xliv), Navy photographer Saundra Spencer was assigned the secret task of developing photographs of the autopsy. She "recalled one photograph showing a blowout or missing area in the center of the back of the President's head in one image, which appeared to be two to two-and-one-half inches wide."

In 1997 the ARRB interviewed a retired federal government civilian photographer, Joe O'Donnell, who knew the official White House photographer in the Kennedy administration, Robert Knudsen, who had told his family before he died that he was involved in taking photographs for the Kennedy autopsy and that he was sworn to secrecy about what he had done. According to Horne (volume 1, page xliv), Knudsen showed O'Donnell two sets of photographs:

One set of images showed a hole in the back of the head about the size of a grapefruit, and an apparent entry wound in the forehead above the right eye, about 3/8 in diameter. A second set of images showed no damage to the rear of the head, and the hair appeared to be wet, and washed, in those photographs.

I probably should also mention that immediately after the assassination, a medical student named William Harper found a section of Kennedy's skull on the grass near where Kennedy was shot. Lifton writes (page 316):

Harper took the bone to Methodist Hospital, where it was examined by Dr. Cairns, the Chief Pathologist. According to an FBI interview, "Dr. Cairns stated the bone specimen looked like it came from the occipital region of the skull." According to Dr. Cairns' identification, the fragment found by William Harper came from the same anatomic location where Dr. McClelland, and many other Dallas observers, saw the wound in the president's head.

THE SHOT THAT KILLED KENNEDY

After the Harper fragment was turned over to the federal officials, they somehow lost it and could never locate it again.

Is there a connection between Kennedy's head wound and the early delivery of Kennedy's body to the Bethesda morgue on the evening of November 22?

The answer to that question is included in a fascinating scenario, initially set forth by David Lifton back in 1981 in his book *Best Evidence* and then later expanded upon by Douglas Horne. That scenario is explored in *The Kennedy Autopsy*.

About the Author

Jacob Hornberger is founder and president of The Future of Freedom Foundation. He was born and raised in Laredo, Texas, and received his B.A. in economics from Virginia Military Institute and his law degree from the University of Texas. He was a trial attorney for twelve years in Texas. He also was an adjunct professor at the University of Dallas, where he taught law and economics. In 1987, Jacob left the practice of law to become director of programs at The Foundation for Economic Education in Irvington-on-Hudson, New York, publisher of *The Freeman.*

In 1989, Jacob founded The Future of Freedom Foundation. He is a regular writer for The Foundation's publication, *The Future of Freedom,* and his editorials have appeared in the *Washington Post, Charlotte Observer, La Prensa San Diego, El Nuevo Miami Herald,* and many others, both in the United States and in Latin America.

Jacob is the author of *The Kennedy Autopsy* and a contributor to *JFK's War with the National Security Establishment: Why Kennedy Was Assassinated* by Douglas Horne. He is also co-editor, along with Richard M. Ebeling, of *Liberty, Security, and the War on Terrorism; The Failure of America's Foreign Wars; The Tyranny of Gun Control; The Case for Free Trade and Open Immigration;* and *The Dangers of Socialized Medicine.* He is also a contributor to the following books authored by Sheldon Richman: *Separating School & State: How to Liberate America's Families; Your Money or Your Life: Why We Should Abolish the Income Tax;* and *Tethered Citizens: Time to Repeal the Welfare State.*

Jacob has delivered speeches and engaged in debates and discussions about free-market principles with groups all over the United States, as well as Canada, England, Europe, and Latin America, including Brazil, Cuba, Bolivia, Mexico, Costa Rica, and Argentina, and he has also advanced freedom and free markets on talk-radio stations all across the country as well as on the FOX News Neil Cavuto, Greta Van Susteren, and Andrew Napolitano shows. He currently participates in the video series *The Libertarian Angle* (archived on YouTube).

Printed in Great Britain
by Amazon

60045793R00072